"Since 1980, I have been turning to the teachings of Steve Brown for encouragement and direction. His words have inspired, encouraged, shocked, and entertained me. He's never boring, always fresh, and most of all, he loves Jesus. This book is a delight and so is its author."
Max Lucado, Pastor; bestselling author of *Glory Days*

"In a society wherein so many of us suffer estrangement from one another because we are prone to be con artists, Steve Brown calls us to become authentic people. With a special gift for saying things that are both profound and punchy, he provides us with a book that will challenge any reader to make a Spirit-filled presentation of self in everyday life that is real. I loved reading this book."
Tony Campolo, Professor Emeritus, Eastern University

"Anxieties thrive when fear of failure and rejection gain a foothold in our hearts. And so we hide behind masks that prevent us from being known and loved just as we are. Steve Brown—one of the most big-hearted pastors I know—is determined to emancipate us from our masks and, in *Hidden Agendas*, guides us into the sanctuary and freedom of God's lavish love and grace. Truly a liberating read!"
Carolyn Custis James, Author of *Malestrom: Manhood Swept into the Currents of a Changing World*

"Wearing the mask of a serious Christian journalist, I say: Here is a profound, engaging, and lived theology of grace that the church desperately needs. Taking off the mask, I say: Thank you, thank you, thank you—here is an invitation to freedom this sinner needs."
Mark Galli, Editor, *Christianity Today*

"As with Lon Chaney in *Phantom of the Opera*, the mask's been ripped off. He screamed when it came down. What will I do? Steve Brown teaches me to sigh with bles   ᵕ ᵕ will the church let me? Steve's church will, and I believ
rific book—every searing word of i
Paul Zahl, Author; retired Epis

"Steve Brown's new book, *Hidden Agendas*, messes with us where we need to be messed with and encourages us to live and love with the freedom that Jesus intends for us. The gospel of God's grace exposes and sabotages all posing and pretending, and Steve helps us understand what that disruptive and liberating process involves. As an adjunct faculty member of five seminaries around the country, this book has vaulted high on my recommended reading list for everybody preparing to serve in some form of vocational ministry, but it's a must-read for all of us who care about making the gospel as beautiful and believable as we possibly can."

Scotty Ward Smith, Teacher in Residence, West End Community Church, Nashville, Tennessee

"Beloved, this book is a treasure. Steve, in his winsome, down-to-earth way frees you from the desire to remain hidden and gently leads you into the truth of who you really are. I found myself laughing one second and weeping for joy the next. Read, rejoice, rest."

Jessica Thompson, Speaker; author of *Everyday Grace*

"Talk about crafty. Under the guise of exploring that scariest of topics, human motivation, Steve Brown has hidden a remarkably wide-ranging, uncommonly funny, and psychologically penetrating masterclass of practical theology. What's more, he's jam-packed it with the kind of stories you can only accumulate from a lifetime of full-blooded ministry, rooting the Good News right where it belongs—behind the masks we all wear. Here's a not-so-hidden, kicker-free agenda for anyone interested in understanding themselves, loving other people, or knowing God. Digest this book, post-haste."

David Zahl, Editor, *The Mockingbird Blog*; author of *A Mess of Help: From the Crucified Soul of Rock n Roll*

HIDDEN AGENDAS

DROPPING THE MASKS THAT KEEP US APART

Steve Brown

New
Growth
Press
WWW.NEWGROWTHPRESS.COM

New Growth Press, Greensboro, NC 27404

Cover Design: Faceout Books, faceoutstudio.com
Typesetting and eBook: Lisa Parnell, lparnell.com

ISBN 978-1-942572-65-7 (Print)
ISBN 978-1-942572-66-4 (eBook)

Library of Congress Cataloging-in-Publication Data
  Names: Brown, Stephen W., author.
  Title: Hidden agendas : dropping the masks that keep us apart /
    Steve Brown.
  Description: Greensboro, NC : New Growth Press, 2016. |
    Includes bibliographical references and index.
  Identifiers: LCCN 2015044399 | ISBN 9781942572657 (print) |
    ISBN 9781942572664 (ebook)
  Subjects: LCSH: Integrity—Religious aspects—Christianity.
  Classification: LCC BV4647.I55 B76 2016 | DDC 248.4—dc23
  LC record available at http://lccn.loc.gov/2015044399

Printed in United States of America

23 22 21 20 19 18 17 16   1 2 3 4 5

Contents

Acknowledgments

So many people helped with this book.

Robin DeMurga should be listed as the coauthor of the book, given the incredible and gifted amount of work she has done with it. The staff at Key Life makes it possible for me to write books and get the credit (or blame) when God knows the truth about the way they "hold up my arms." And the people at New Growth Press are the best. So many have taught me, advised me, corrected me, and guided me that they are too numerous to mention.

Without all of those people, this book would have been far worse . . .

. . . or maybe better.

Introduction

"You haven't lived long enough or sinned big enough to even have an opinion on that!"

That's what I sometimes say to seminary students who have a tendency to be overly critical of others and are terribly sure of their own ability to discern truth.

It's true about books too. There are certain kinds of books that one shouldn't write until one has lived long enough and sinned big enough. I've lived long enough and I've sinned big enough to write this book, and so it's time.

My friend John Frost, one of the most brilliant programmers of contemporary Christian music stations in the country, often consults with the ministry where I work. Not too long ago, he told me that he had finally figured me out. He said, "Steve, you don't care."

He was at least partially right. When you're old, you really don't care about some things (though you do find yourself caring more about others). I don't care who Lady Gaga is sleeping with or what's happening with Miley Cyrus. Facebook doesn't keep me up at night, and I don't give a rip about who's tweeting on Twitter or posting stuff on Instagram. I honestly couldn't care less about what Brad Pitt thinks or how much weight Oprah Winfrey loses.

I've also found that, as I get older, I don't care much about what people think about me either. As I age, I've found that I'm harder to manipulate; that leverage doesn't work with me the way it once did. If you're "cramming for finals," you have a perspective that you don't have when you're young.

That means this book will be relatively honest.

Dr. House (of television fame) often says, "Everybody lies." That may be truer than any of us would like to admit. But when one gets as old as I am, one lies less and, more important for the purpose of this book, one doesn't feel as constrained to wear so many masks. It may or may not be true that everybody lies, but everybody wears a mask, everybody has an agenda, and almost everybody you know is different than you think.

Did you hear about the woman who went to the hospital for a fairly difficult surgery? While on the operating table, she had a near-death experience and encountered God. She asked him if it was her time to die. God said that it wasn't and she would, in fact, live for another forty-three years. Sure enough, she got through the surgery successfully. While still recovering in the hospital, since she now knew she was going to live a long time, the woman decided to have some cosmetic procedures done. She got a facelift and a tummy tuck and even brought in a stylist to give her a whole new hairstyle and color.

On the day she left the hospital, the woman felt like a million bucks. But as she crossed the street to the parking lot, she was struck by a truck and killed.

Introduction

When the woman stood before God, she was quite upset. "I thought you told me I would live for another forty-three years. How could you do this to me?"

"To be perfectly honest," God said, "I didn't recognize you."

In reality, God always recognizes us. He sees behind the masks we wear and the hidden agendas that drive us. It does no good for you to tell God that you're sick when you're drunk, that you love him when you don't, or that you didn't steal and eat an apple . . . with apple juice dripping down your chin. So sometimes (not always) we're reasonably honest with God, but it will be a cold day in a hot place before most of us will be fully honest with anybody else. God, of course, isn't that safe, but his job description is love.

The rest of the world scares the spit out of us.

I have suggested in a number of places (books, broadcasts, sermons, and lectures) that all Christian authors should be required to confess their sins in the first chapter of their books. That way, it would lend credence and power to whatever else they wrote. Too often truth is obscured because the writer seems to speak from Sinai, though, of course, nobody but God does.

So before we go any further, I need to say something: *I'm sometimes so phony I can hardly stand myself.*

I'm not proud of that; in fact, it embarrasses me to say it. I'm not even sure I would say it if it weren't for a truth I learned from a whole lot of years of working with people: *You're just as phony as I am.*

So I've lived long enough and I've sinned big enough to write this book. Nobody is going to fire me, I have enough money to pay the mortgage and to take my wife out to dinner, and I'm not looking for anything from anybody. That means I'm going to tell you the truth about me (within certain limits of propriety) and about you.

Let's talk.

CHAPTER 1

Halloween Horror

Therefore, having this ministry by the mercy of God, we do not lose heart. But we have renounced disgraceful, underhanded ways. We refuse to practice cunning or to tamper with God's word, but by the open statement of the truth, we would commend ourselves to everyone's conscience in the sight of God. (2 Corinthians 4:1–2)

A number of years ago I left the pastorate of a church I loved because the church almost killed me. (That may be a bit harsh, given that I did a lot of the killing of myself.) I was very close to an emotional meltdown and nobody knew it. If you have a deep and authoritative voice (and I do), degrees from academic institutions (and I do), a reputation for competence (and I did), and you write books (I still do), people figure you're okay and, in fact, come to you for help so they can be okay too.

But "the wheels were coming off my wagon" and I didn't even know it.

It was late at night and I was alone in my study. There was nobody to impress, nobody to convince, and nobody to encourage when, to my total surprise and for no apparent reason, I began to sob. I found myself saying out loud (also a surprise), "I don't want to do this anymore. In fact, I can't do this anymore." The next day I resigned as the pastor of that church and started a very long journey (which still continues) to find out what was wrong with me. For the next year I talked to friends and counselors, read a pile of books, listened to hours of recorded lectures, and, in the quiet, I thought about me, about God, and about the life that had become such a burden.

There's an old Sunday school song that children still sing (a play on the nursery rhyme, "If you're happy and you know it . . ."): "If you're saved and you know it, clap your hands. If you're saved and you know it, then your life will surely show it. Clap your hands!"

Let me tweak that song a bit. "If you're a sinner and you know it, then your life should really show it." If you like singing those kinds of songs, you can even expand it: "If you're needy, or afraid, or lonely, or confused, or ashamed, or depressed, or in pain, then your life should really show it. Clap your hands."

For the rest of this book, we're going to put legs on that song. A good place to begin is to define the questions, such as:

- What is a hidden agenda and why is it hidden?
- What are masks and why do we wear them?
- How do those masks and agendas hurt us and those we love?

- Why are we so afraid that people will discover our agendas and look behind our masks?

Have you ever noticed what the neighbors of serial killers say to reporters? It's generally some form of surprise as in, "I just don't understand . . . he liked kittens and children. He seemed like such a nice man." I believe that, in a different context, almost all of our neighbors, friends, acquaintances, and fellow Christians would say the same thing. But I have a pastor friend who told his congregation, "If you knew me—I mean *really* knew me—you wouldn't want me to be your pastor." Then he smiled and said, "If I knew you—I mean *really* knew you—frankly, I wouldn't want you to be my congregation." In that mildly humorous comment there is profound wisdom.

I'm a religious professional, and because I have a media ministry, people who know about me generally only know the public image they hear on radio, see on television, and encounter on our website. Not only that, I write religious books. When I speak at a church, seminar, or conference, there is always a space between where I stand and the people who listen. (Someone has said, "In the church they put the pastors six feet above everybody else, shine a spotlight on them, give them a microphone, and tell them to be humble.")

You have no idea how often I've said, "If they only knew."

If you've ever said or thought, "If they only knew," what I'm going to show you will be helpful and freeing. It might even change your life. But we have miles to go before we get there. What follows in this chapter is a boring but necessary first step.

What Is a Hidden Agenda and Why Is It Hidden?

An "agenda" is a plan designed to accomplish, change, fix, destroy, remedy, reward, punish, promote, or hinder. In other words, an agenda is what we do to get from where we are to where we want to be—from here to there. Further, a hidden agenda is either hidden intentionally to accomplish what we desire, or hidden unintentionally because we don't even know we have an agenda in the first place.

For years I've taught ecclesiastical politics to seminary students. It started in a faculty meeting after a discussion of why so many of our students were being "chewed up" by some people in the church. Most of God's people—some 90 percent—are kind, gentle, loving, and affirming. But the remaining 10 percent are some of the meanest, most condemning, and most destructive people you can imagine. Those 10 percent are the ones with "hidden agendas" geared, for whatever reason, to hurt the pastor. At the seminary we decided we had done well in biblical studies, theology, and counseling, but we had never taught our students survival techniques. Because that particular subject had not been taught, our graduates, now in ministry, were being drawn and quartered, and didn't even know what was happening.

(As an aside, that 90/10 principle—90 percent normal, affirming, and kind; and 10 percent neurotic and mean as snakes—is applicable to almost any human institution. It's not that the church is worse than any other institution. But even though the church is a lot more than an institution, it *is* an institution and operates under the same basic principles as any institution.)

Since I teach practical theology, the faculty decided I should address the problem. So I designed several lectures designed to prepare students on how, as Jesus put it, to be "as wise as serpents and innocent as doves" (Matthew 10:16). Those lectures included such subjects as identifying "pockets of power" and how to deal with them, how to develop a godly "mean" streak, how to win battles without losing one's salvation, how to count votes, how to deal with criticism, how to be sensitive and aware of trends in the church, when to confront and when to remain silent, etc.

Students didn't like those lectures and complained loudly about them. They called what I taught "manipulative" and "unchristian." My response was always, "I don't care what you think. You will listen and you will be tested on this material. I'm teaching you stuff that will save your ministry. One day you will 'rise up and call me blessed.'"

You would be surprised by how often those students do "rise up and call me blessed." So often I'll get a call, email, or letter from a former student who says, "Steve, I want to ask you to forgive me. I repent of what I said about your teaching on church politics. What you taught me saved my ministry [generally they say "butt" . . . however, that isn't appropriate for a Christian book] and I wanted to say thank you."

What was I doing in those lectures? I taught students to have an agenda and, for the most part, it was a hidden agenda. For those of you who are shocked at what I just wrote, I also taught them to do it for the glory of Christ, and the peace and unity of the church.

However, there is more. The 90 percent (the kind and gentle ones in the church) have an agenda too. It's just not as destructive as the other 10 percent. Nevertheless, agendas are a part of us all. When I went through the emotional meltdown I described earlier, I found that almost all of the pain I went through was due to my own agendas, and those agendas had become the "stuff" out of which I made masks—professional, religious, personal, relational, and so on. In the pages that follow I'll reference my own agendas (mostly hidden, and probably not dissimilar to yours) and look at finding a road to make those agendas less destructive, more authentic, and incredibly freeing.

What Are Masks and Why Do We Wear Them?

Masks are designed to hide, conceal, or disguise the reality behind them. In other words, the masks are created to further an agenda. Like any agenda, the masks are sometimes intentional, but more often than not, the wearers are unaware of their masks.

Someone has said that the definition of "diplomacy" is saying "Nice dog . . . nice dog" until you get a stick. The "nice dog" part is the mask.

Christians are masters at hidden agendas and masks. We'll talk a lot more about that later, but for now, let's acknowledge that, depending on your definition of the Christian faith, a mask may seem necessary. The church, properly defined, is a hospital, among other things. When people join the church, they have made a public statement that they are needy, sinful, and desperate. And the Bible teaches that while we generally do get better, the need, sin, and desperation are ongoing realities.

The problem occurs when church people redefine the church as a gathering of "fixed" people who are good, together, and better than the cretins who aren't in the church. Because that is not the biblical reality, those who define the church that way must create an "image" of what is not the reality. That "image" is the mask. If we wear the mask long enough, we begin to think that the mask is the reality.

My pastor recently read us the welcome message from Our Lady of Lourdes Catholic Church in Daytona Beach, Florida:

> We extend a special welcome to those who are single, married, divorced, filthy rich, dirt poor, *y no habla Ingles*. We extend a special welcome to those who are crying newborns, skinny as a rail, or could afford to lose a few pounds. We welcome you if you can sing like Andrea Bocelli, or like our pastor, who can't carry a note in a bucket. You're welcome here if you're "just browsing," just woke up, or just got out of jail. . . . We extend a special welcome to those who are over sixty but not grown up yet, and to teenagers who are growing up too fast. We welcome soccer moms, NASCAR dads, starving artists, tree-huggers, latte-sippers, vegetarians, junk-food eaters. We welcome those who are in recovery or are still addicted. We welcome you if you're having problems, or you're down in the dumps, or if you don't like "organized religion" (we've been there, too). If you blew all your offering money at the dog track, you're welcome here. . . . We welcome those who are inked, pierced, or both. We offer a special welcome to those who could use a prayer right now, had religion shoved down your throat as a kid, or got lost in traffic and wound up here by mistake. . . . We welcome tourists, seekers, doubters, bleeding hearts . . . and you.[1]

In other words, you're welcome here to take off your masks and come as you are. The problem is that taking off our masks is not as easy as accepting an invitation to church. It can be quite dangerous.

In one old *Barney Miller* TV episode, the police commissioner required the detectives to wear uniforms most of the week. One of the detectives complained to his sergeant, "If we start wearing uniforms, people will start thinking we know what we're doing and, even worse, *we'll* start thinking we know what we are doing. That could be dangerous."

There are a great variety of masks—religious masks, power masks, protective masks, professional masks, and political masks. Some are designed to promote a political agenda or to hide fear. Other masks are designed to create fear. Some masks garner power or money. Some masks are created to solicit from others compassion and mercy, or to fake compassion and mercy. There are "coping" masks that enable us to function. And of course there are piles of religious masks that fake a walk with God . . . not the reality. The list goes on and on; but for now, it is sufficient to understand the basic nature of the mask.

There is one other thing. I mentioned in the introduction that Dr. House said that everybody lies. I'm not sure I totally agree with Dr. House . . . but close. At any rate, I know that I have been known to lie and everybody I know has the same problem. (No, I'm not advocating lying.) I'm not proud of that and repent of it when I see it in myself, but the truth—the whole truth and nothing but the truth—is a hard thing to come by. But even if everybody doesn't lie, everybody does wear a mask that is, by its definition, something not true. (And by the way, masks are sometimes necessary. I'll address that subject in another chapter.)

1. Why are we so afraid that people will discover our agendas and look behind our masks?

Because we are ashamed, dummy.

There are, I'm told, four great adult fears: fear of rejection, fear of failure, fear of punishment, and fear of shame. We wear masks because of one form or another of those fears. If I take off my mask and show you the way I really am, I'm afraid you won't like (love) me. Behind the mask is the reality that sometimes I don't have the foggiest idea of what I'm doing. If you see behind the mask, you will know that I'm a failure and I will fail. I'm not a good person and certainly not as good as my mask would suggest, so removing the mask will exact a price. My shame defines me—what I've done, where I've gone, what I think, who I am—and I just don't think I can stand more shame once you know what's behind the mask.

You've heard of Maslow's four levels of learning: (1) unconscious incompetency, (2) conscious incompetency, (3) conscious competency, and (4) unconscious competency. In other words, (1) we don't know that we don't know, (2) then we know we don't know, (3) then we know, and (4) finally we know and don't even think about it.

It's the same way with masks. At a certain point in our lives, we are unaware that the world is an unsafe place where we can be rejected, fail, be punished, and be shamed. When the reality of an unsafe world begins to emerge in the socialization process of "growing up," we create ways to deal with the danger. We do that with masks, and there is a degree of intentionality involved. Then, as we become more and more socialized, we don't even know who we are anymore. And, of course, the danger is that we become, in fact, the very masks we wear.

So we're afraid of taking off the masks not just because of what's under them, but because we instinctively know that our masks have become so much a part of us that to exorcise them would go to the core of who we are. That scares the spit out of us.

In Dave Eggers's novel, *The Circle*, Mae Holland is hired to work for The Circle, which has become (or is becoming) the most powerful internet company in the world. The Circle is on a wonderful, very large campus in California, where every aspect of their employees' lives is affirmed, encouraged, supported, lavishly compensated . . . and public. Mae is discovered to have stolen (rationalized as "borrowed") a kayak out for an evening trip on the ocean. It's a long scene but eventually she is shamed into confessing her sins and her "individual" indulgence. Slowly and surely she "sells her soul to the company store." At first she is aware of what is happening, but eventually she becomes a model company employee, even (and I don't want to spoil the story for you) betraying others in the most brutal and destructive way. The scary part is that, all the while, Mae really believes she is making a positive contribution to the company and the world.[2]

That's what happens with the masks we wear. They slowly become what we think is the reality of who we are. It's hard to see that, in fact, we're hiding behind a mask.

2. Where did we learn to create hidden agendas and to wear masks?

That question presupposes what I believe to be a very naïve view of human nature. That naïveté is the source of an almost universal (but spurious) belief about human goodness. It comes from the same place as the lieutenant's song in *South Pacific*. He is facing devastating prejudice and sings that human beings have to be "carefully taught to hate." No, actually, they don't. Biblical anthropology teaches that you don't have to be taught to hate or, for that matter, to be phony or to use a mask to pursue a hidden and mostly selfish agenda. It's normal, natural, and quite scary.

Of course, all of us watch and learn. We learn from those who manipulate us for their own agenda and who themselves have been manipulated by others to further their agendas. It is as old as mankind and goes back to a man by the name of Adam who wore the first mask when he "covered himself" with fig leaves. You remember the incident. It's in the Bible (Genesis 3) where Adam's disobedience led to awareness, his awareness led to shame, and his shame led to the fig leaf mask. When God showed up, he called out to Adam, "Where are you?" Adam hid . . . and we've been hiding ever since.

You're bent. I'm bent. The world is bent. And so we hide.

Once we start to understand the nature of hidden agendas and the masks we wear to cover them, we sometimes begin to think that if there were a pristine goodness, purity, and unselfishness in us, the "true self" would be that. I've read a number of books in preparation for writing this one and many of them make that assumption. They say that underneath the mask and behind the hidden agenda is a really nice and loving person who is the "real you" or, as one writer puts it, "the true self." That's a seductive message but it is one that can kill you if you let it because it simply isn't true. More than that, the process of getting to the "true you" isn't pleasant, because the "true you" is often no better than the "false you." Sometimes it is far worse.

"He seems to be a really nasty man," someone said of a mutual acquaintance, "but underneath it, he is worse than he seems." That could be, believe it or not, true to one degree or another of all of us. The myth that children start out good and become bad is just that—a myth. A friend recently sent me the definition of a "toddler": "Noun. Emotionally unstable, pint-sized dictator with the uncanny ability to know exactly how far to push you into utter insanity before reverting to a lovable child." It starts that way and it never stops. The difference is that socialization teaches us to hide it. That's the true source of most masks.

While that may be cynical (I am, after all, an old, cynical preacher), I don't think so. In fact, it is both good news and bad news, and we'll talk more about it later.

3. Then why even bother to get rid of the masks or to reveal the agendas in the first place?

That's a good question. If things are the way I've described them—if masks are our protection, and if revealing what's behind our masks is so painful—why even go to the trouble?

Let me tell you why. There is so much more to life than hiding, pretending, and never being loved. There's also the horrible loneliness of shame, and it's killing us. In fact, that's what the Christian faith is all about—sinful, lonely, and needy people meeting and loving other sinful, lonely, and needy people. And when we do so, it changes the narrative . . . and thus changes the world.

Take the time sometime to read through the Bible. If you never have, you're going to discover things you wouldn't believe would be in any holy book. You'll find murderers and whores, liars and thieves, con artists and hypocrites, whiners and manipulators, power-hungry tyrants and dishonest, selfish, and arrogant leaders. The most stunning thing is that, in almost all these cases, they are the leaders of

God's people, the first recipients of the covenant with God, and the preachers and teachers of the message of Christ.

What's going on? They are ripping off their masks (or maybe God is doing it for them) for one reason: a message from God, telling his creation that the only way to get to a life worth living, to experience love worth having, and to be free to laugh, sing, and dance is to get rid of the masks and to be honest about the agendas. You see, God has this proclivity—this strong inclination—when it comes to those he loves. His proclivity is to rip off the masks in direct proportion to our proclivity to wear them.

Is everything going to be fixed once we take off our masks? Are you crazy? That's just plain utopian (and truth be told, more damage has been done by utopians than you can imagine). But things have got to be better than they are, at least within the household of God. The world desperately needs to hear the "laughter of the redeemed." That will never happen until the redeemed risk everything and discover they are free. "Free at last! Free at last! Thank God Almighty, I'm free at last."

4. Why do the masks and hidden agendas hurt us and those we love?

We hurt ourselves and those we love because love isn't love until it's love that takes place within the context of the unlovely. If you're not a drunk, you'll never know the fellowship—honest, free, and joyful—of drunks who know it but find themselves loved. If you don't think you're a sinner, you'll never dance before the throne of the Redeemer. If you don't see how needy you are, you'll never know the absolute and pure joy of being free with others who admit it and are free.

Mother Teresa once wrote, "The greatest disease in the West today is not TB or leprosy; it is being unwanted, unloved, and uncared for. We can cure physical diseases with medicine, but the only cure for loneliness, despair, and hopelessness is love. There are many in the world who are dying for a piece of bread but there are many more dying for a little love. The poverty in the West is a different kind of poverty—it is not only a poverty of loneliness but also of spirituality. There's a hunger for love, as there is a hunger for God. . . . 'We must be loved by God first, and only then can we give it to others. For us to want to give love to others we must be full of love to give.'"[3]

We live in a reward-based culture. Do it right and it will come out right. Other than the fact that it's not true, it really does sound good. After all, if we studied hard, we got good grades. If we worked hard, we got a promotion. If we were nice, people were nice to us. Never mind that sometimes our friend cheated and got good grades, or we worked hard and had a teacher who was a twit and didn't understand how profound our answers to the test really were. Maybe we discovered that there were a whole lot of people who were simply mean to the bone and, no matter how nice we were, they would never return the favor. But even if that's true (and it is), we still believe that if you do it right, it will turn out right. So we work hard, live pure, and are nice. When it turns out that we can't work that hard, live that pure, or be that nice, we create a mask. The mask reflects our shame and the horrible fear that others will see. Then we become "islands" unto ourselves, lonely, fearful, and guilty.

But what if we said, "I'm not playing that game anymore, even if nothing turns out right"? Let me tell you what would happen: love would happen. We would discover that

God hugs dirty kids. Then love would happen to us from God and from us to others. It wouldn't be the phony love that is given in response to being good, pure, successful, nice, and strong. That's not love; that's reward. In fact, you can't know love until you know you don't deserve it. In other words, you can't know love until you are willing to risk getting it by taking off the mask. And within the context of that kind of love, the list of gifts God gives to those who are unmasked is incredibly long. We'll be talking about that list.

5. So how do we deal with our masks?

You die! That's what you do.

I know, I know. That's not very good news. It really isn't but it becomes the good news—incredibly good news—as it's lived. If I had an alternative title to this book, I guess it would be *How to Die and Have Fun Doing It.*

But before we go there, I feel constrained to say some positive things about masks. The road we are going to take over the next few chapters will make you weird if you don't read the next chapter. So do that and then we'll get back to the subject at hand.

Behind the Mask

1. What is the purpose of masks and hidden agendas?
2. Why are masks and hidden agendas so common in the church?
3. Do you think you have a hidden agenda and wear a mask (or masks)? While you may be unaware of them, make a guess.
4. Describe a situation in which you were hurt by a friend's mask or hidden agenda. How did you feel?

5. What would happen if your masks and hidden agendas were stripped away? What would be left? What are you afraid of?

Background Scriptures: 2 Corinthians 4:1–2; Genesis 3

Note to small group leaders: Refer to these Scriptures as needed during your discussion, along with Scripture passages in this chapter.

CHAPTER 2

Ugly in a Nudist Colony

"Do not give dogs what is holy, and do not throw your pearls before pigs, lest they trample them underfoot and turn to attack you." (Matthew 7:6)

A number of years ago I was the host of a fairly "edgy" daily Christian talk show. It didn't last very long because Christians don't do edgy very well. While the talk show had a serious purpose to it, we did a lot of comedy (Christians don't do that very well either). Someone told our producer about a "Christian" nudist colony in our area, so we decided to send some of the staff to check it out. We sent two guys whose wives wouldn't let them go unless they (the wives) went with them. I suppose the wives had visions of erotic scenes with sexy women running around naked, and that was just not something they could sanction . . . at least not unless they were there.

Their fears were misplaced.

It turned out to be a funny, interesting, and controversial segment, but do you know the most interesting thing about the report? It was how ugly the nudists were. It's not that Christian nudists are particularly ugly or more ugly than the average Christian with clothes on, it was just that those things that make ugly less ugly (i.e., clothes) were set aside.

Just as clothes have a purpose, so do masks. My late mentor, Fred Smith, once said that the reckless ripping off of a mask is the kiss of death for friendship. He was right. Ripping off masks at the wrong time, in the wrong place, and with the wrong people is not only the death for friendship, it can cause great damage.

So before we do anything else, I want to begin with a word of caution.

Years ago a friend gave me a copy of *Gracian's Manual: A Truth-Telling Manual and the Art of Worldly Wisdom.* It is a compilation of the rather cynical and sometimes wise words written by a seventeenth-century Spanish Jesuit. This is what Gracian wrote about masks:

> He is not a fool who commits foolishness, but he who having done so does not know how to conceal it. If your merits should be kept under seal, how much more your demerits. All men go wrong; but with this difference, the intelligent cover up what they have committed, and the fools expose even what they may commit. A good name rests more upon what is concealed, than upon what is revealed, for he who cannot be good, must be cautious. . . . Let it be a mistake to confide your errors even to a friend, for were it possible, you should not disclose them to yourself; but since this is

impossible, make use here of that other principle of life, which is: learn how to forget.[1]

I'm going to spend much of this book telling you why Gracian was wrong, but do let me first tell you why he was (and is) right.

I teach at a seminary where students are trained for ministry. In my courses I talk about the changes that have taken place in our culture (sometimes called "postmodernity") and what is now required of those who would communicate to that culture. The cultural shift has brought some good things and some not-so-good things to the preacher. Christians no longer have the money, leverage, favor, and political power we once had. That's bad. Actually, no, it's a gift. Now instead of using inappropriate and sometimes sinful tools to communicate the verities of the Christian faith, we have to do it the way Jesus did it. He didn't have money, leverage, favor, or political power either.

One of the catchwords of our changing culture is "authenticity." I've grown to dislike that word. It's overused, hardly ever defined, and sometimes has become a cliché. However, the word does reflect an important principle of communication to people who live in our culture, to wit, if you aren't the "real deal," nobody will pay attention to anything you say.

So I teach my students to be authentic. I tell them, "If you can learn to fake authenticity, people will listen." Of course not! I teach them to be honest and open about who they really are, the struggles and sins they have, and the pain they experience. I will often say to my students, "Nobody speaks from Sinai, and when you appear to be an outsider to the human race, you truncate the message you communicate. You need forgiveness and encouragement as much as anybody. You need to cut some slack for the people you serve and they need to cut some slack for you."

My late friend, Jack Miller (founder of World Harvest Mission—now called Serge—and originator of the *Sonship* course), often said that the most repentant person in any congregation should be the pastor.

But with all that being said, I have found that I have to give those students the same advice I'm going to give you: You be careful out there. If the church were what it is supposed to be—a fellowship of brutally honest sinners who love one another and taste the salt of one another's tears— you wouldn't have to be careful. But the church is a whore even if she is also your mother (as Augustine suggested). So often the church is simply not a safe place. So don't be so honest that you lose your job, cause the leadership to wonder if you're saved, or cause your mother to blush. That's good advice for everybody. You be careful out there too.

The denomination of which I'm a part is divided into presbyteries. A presbytery is a group of church pastors and leaders who live in a defined geographical area. Generally, while presbyteries are necessary for a lot of reasons, the meetings are boring, anal, and so often "the noise of solemn assemblies." Nobody I know likes presbytery meetings . . . well, nobody "normal," that is.

A number of years ago, some of the young leaders in our presbytery decided they weren't going to (and couldn't) stand for it anymore. They took over our presbytery and one of the leaders announced that it was a new day with, "We need each other and, from now on, we are going to be different. We're going to devote presbytery meetings to caring for and loving each other instead of just church business.

And this morning we are going to begin by confessing our sins to one another. I'll start."

Then to the shock and surprise of everybody there, that leader confessed a very embarrassing and particularly humiliating sin to the presbytery. "Now," he said, "it's your turn."

There was a long pause and then, to my surprise, members of presbytery stood up and one by one confessed their sins. Those weren't the "deep and dark" sins over which Christians crucify other Christians, but it was a good and freeing beginning.

I was sitting in the back of the auditorium when all of this happened. As the confession progressed, I noticed that the presbytery members kept turning around and looking at me. I had been a seminary professor to many of them and it was apparent to me that they could hardly wait to get some dirt on the old guy.

So finally I stood up. It grew so quiet that you could hear a flea burp. In my kind and pastoral way I said, "Are you crazy? I'm not confessing my sins to this bunch. You aren't that safe! So forget it." Then I sat down, only to quickly stand back up again and say, "Well, I suppose that is a sort of confession."

Everybody laughed because we all knew that, while confession was good for the soul and good for the church, inappropriate confession was quite dangerous.

We live in a time when secrets are hard to keep. With social media, cameras on every corner, YouTube, email hackers, and viral tweets, town gossips have pretty much been put out of business—or maybe now they have a much bigger platform. If you don't want everyone to know what you say, write, and do, don't say it, don't write it, and don't do it. It will come back to bite you. Just ask those whose lives were destroyed by an online revelation, a Google search, or a camera about which they were unaware.

Until the church, the world, and our communities become safe places, a wise man or woman will be careful about an inappropriate authenticity that is more akin to stripping than honesty. So before we "get down" to our discussion of masks and how they hurt us and those we love, let me remind you of some things that are very important.

The Importance of Timing

First, don't forget the importance of *timing*. When Jesus washed the disciples' feet, he said that the disciples didn't understand what he was doing "now, but afterward you will understand" (John 13:7). Then later in John, Jesus said, "I still have many things to say to you, but you cannot bear them now" (John 16:12). Jesus is talking about timing.

The late George Buttrick, the minister at Madison Avenue Presbyterian Church in New York, used to say that there are some things a preacher can't say to a congregation until he's been with them a year and other things he can't say until he's been there twenty years. That's true of preachers but it's also true of us all. There is a process of "soul trading" that must always be respected.

Among other things, what lies behind the mask we show to the world is our soul, the essence of who we really are. It's the hidden places of our lives. "Soul trading" is what happens in a marriage and it can become, if one isn't careful, a suicide pact. After a short time a husband and wife know each other in ways that nobody else can. In this process of soul-trading, they learn how to build up and encourage, and also how to destroy and discourage. When a marriage is a good one, what is acquired during the soul-trading process becomes the "stuff" out of which solid marriages are built. On the other hand, in a bad marriage there is more pain and destruction than in almost any other relationship for the same reason. For instance, when you see a wife demean her husband or a husband his wife, they are using the weapons of destruction acquired in the soul-trading process.

During our lifetimes we are fortunate if we have four or five very close and intimate friends with whom we don't have to pretend. They become that through the soul-trading process, in which each will share or trade small portions of his or her soul in exchange for small portions of the other's soul. In that process, one discerns what the other will do with those small pieces of one's soul. Will the other value, treasure, and affirm the soul or will the other "stomp that sucker flat"? When the response is positive, it is an indication that it's safe for more of one's soul to be traded. The culmination of the process is a soft place in which one can safely remove the mask.

Here is the point. If the process is interrupted or rushed so that real trust and intimacy are only developed superficially (or not at all), the destruction and pain that can result are almost beyond repair. It's what the psalmist was talking about when he wrote, "For it is not an enemy who taunts me—then I could bear it; it is not an adversary who deals insolently with me—then I could hide from him. But it is you, a man, my equal, my companion, my familiar friend. We used to take sweet counsel together; within God's house we walked in the throng" (Psalm 55:12–14).

Removing a mask before it's time is dangerous in a variety of human institutions and relationships. That is especially true in the church because the "institutional mask" is often one of safety and love when just the opposite is true. You may have heard about the small group Bible study

27

where the members decided to trust one another by following the James 5 admonition to "confess your sins to one another." They each confessed their sins: lying, sexual sin, stealing, greed. One man was silent and when he finally spoke, everyone was shocked and one lady fainted. "I have always struggled," he said, "with the sin of gossip, and I must confess that I'm not sure I can keep what I've heard this evening to myself."

You be careful out there.

The Value of Propriety

Timing is important when one is thinking about removing the masks and revealing the hidden agendas but, second, *propriety* is important too. Proverbs 15:23 says, "To make an apt answer is a joy to a man, and a word in season, how good it is!"

Rose Marie Miller is my friend and my hero. Her late husband Jack taught me about grace and she continues to remind me. She's a missionary, a wonderful writer and teacher, and she's in her nineties. She also doesn't very often wear a mask.

Not too long ago she came to Orlando where I live and spoke at a church here. My wife and I went, thinking that Rose Marie would talk about her mission work, the wonderful ways God is honoring that work, and perhaps even ask for support. None of that happened. Instead she confessed her sins. Rose Marie said to the congregation, "I need to say something to you. I have a lady who works with me and she is wonderful. Everybody loves her and she is such a blessing to me. People are attracted to her. The other day, I realized they were attracted to her more than to me. I found myself being jealous and I don't know what to do about it. Would you pray for me?"

My first thought was, *I don't believe I would have said that.* My second thought was a prayer. I thanked God for her, for her authenticity, and for the fact that she was such a gift to all of us. Most of the time, missionaries make me feel guilty because, I suppose, they feel guilty—and/or I'm less committed and spiritual than they are. I know that I sometimes have that effect on people too. Rose Marie reminded me that God loved me with all my humanness and sin. We all need to be reminded.

Sometimes I write to Rose Marie. One time I ended my letter with, "Rose Marie, I prayed for you this morning. Don't screw it up!"

When she wrote back, Rose Marie ended her own letter with, "Thank you for your prayers and I'll try not to *mess* it up." That's when I realized that Rose Marie prefers not to use the words "screw it up" and she had gently reminded me of that fact. I used to teach communication seminars with R. C. Sproul. One of his rules about communication and language is that one should never use words that refer to bodily parts or functions.

There are some things that are appropriate and some things that aren't. In Luke 7 there is a story about a forgiven prostitute who crashed a Pharisee's dinner party. She was not only a prostitute, she was a dumb prostitute. In her line of work, it's best not to show up at a party for Pharisees. I get that she desperately wanted to see Jesus, but if she had been "street smart," she would have waited until after the party and met Jesus as he was leaving. She didn't do that. She came right in. She fell at his feet, worshiped him, and anointed him with precious oil. It's an amazing story and a wonderful one. Jesus accepted her, loved her, and used her as an example of what forgiveness and acceptance meant.

But then, that was Jesus. He's always safe.

So if you're a prostitute, a liar, a sinner, or an adulterer, if you've been unfaithful, hurt people, or stolen from a bank (and we're all one of those), you have to be careful about what you say and where you say it. Some things just aren't appropriate for some people. I teach seminary students (and I'm going to teach you a good deal of the same in this book) to be authentic and real, and to never pretend to be something they aren't. "But," I often say, "be careful about details. Don't do or say anything to a congregation that will cause you to lose your job unless you're absolutely sure God told you to do or say it."

You be careful out there.

The Need for Necessity

Third, timing and propriety are important, but *necessity* is too. The psalmist said, "For he knows the secrets of the heart" (Psalm 44:21). While that's true, it certainly doesn't mean that everybody else should know.

A number of years ago Key Life (the ministry with which I'm involved) conducted *Born Free* seminars at various cities around the country. It is a mix of teaching (mostly from me), drama (with dramatists Charlie and Ruth Jones), and music (with Buddy Greene, the Nashville recording artist). At the heart of the seminar is a major effort at honesty and authenticity. I wrote most of the material after the emotional meltdown I described earlier. In the seminar I try to be as honest as possible about my "stuff," my issues, and my sin.

My late mother had always been horrified when she would listen to my sermons or read one of my books. She once said to her Sunday school class, "All my life I've tried to hide the family secrets and now I have a son who is out telling the whole world." I understood her discomfort. For years before her death—as she listened to the program on her local radio station—I gave instructions to the program producers to leave what I said alone even when I said stupid things. "But," I instructed, "if I ever curse or say anything that would hurt or offend my mother, edit that out."

(As an aside, I wondered what I was going to do with the material in the *Born Free* seminar once we started teaching it around the country. My mother passed away two weeks before that first *Born Free* seminar . . . and I was at her bedside. I wanted to call everybody I knew and say, "Come and watch a godly woman die." She shined and now she's Home. She doesn't mind so much now that I tell the family secrets.)

Sometimes there are people who don't need to see what is behind our masks. When Jesus said in Matthew 7:6 that we shouldn't cast our pearls before swine, he was talking about necessity, among other things. There are people who are so into lying that they lie when the truth would have served them better. And just so, there are people who tell the truth and all the truth when silence would have served them far better as well.

Your casual acquaintances don't need to know your sins. Your mother doesn't need to know things that would shock and disturb her. Your coworker doesn't need to know every thought you think and every stupid thing you've done. There are levels of relationships that grow and flourish with authentic self-revelation, but remember that you don't have to tell the world everything. "That's more than I wanted to know" is the reaction of a benevolent stranger to our authenticity. The others will beat you over the head and try to destroy you with it.

You be careful out there.

The Importance of Details

There is one other caution that I need to share. It is the importance of *details*. When Paul wanted to reach out to his Christian family at the church at Corinth, he wrote, "For we do not want you to be unaware, brothers, of the affliction we experienced in Asia. For we were so utterly burdened beyond our strength that we despaired of life itself" (2 Corinthians 1:8). Paul wanted to "do life together" in such a way that those before whom he removed his mask would know the truth of the life he lived.

This morning I was reading the unpublished manuscript of a friend of mine, once one of the pastors of a large and flourishing congregation. My friend sinned and, when he did, they kicked him out and removed him from the fellowship of the church. His manuscript is not condemning and quite thoughtful. He said that nobody knew him, understood what he was going through, or even asked. F. B. Meyer was a nineteenth-century English pastor and evangelist, and a contemporary and friend of D. L. Moody and Charles Spurgeon. He once said that we should be merciful to those who have sinned because we don't know how hard they tried not to sin nor the forces arrayed against them before they sinned.

That is what church is supposed to be. It's supposed to consist of people who are in such a deep relationship with others that no sin is a surprise or shock, no pain is suffered in private, and no fear is ever faced alone. But we're not there yet.

I have a very close friend who died last week. His death may have been a suicide and I'm afraid to ask. He was one of the most gifted and brilliant men I have ever known . . . and also a drunk. He'd been a drunk almost all his life. My friend's marriage ended in divorce. He told me that his ex-wife was the only woman he ever knew who loved him without condition and that he had destroyed her. He had gone from the pinnacle of his profession to joblessness, homelessness, and despair. Shortly before his death, he had been at a family gathering and was so in need of a drink that he drank the hand sanitizer in the bathroom and, in fact, made a fool of himself.

Years ago my friend said that the reason I liked him was because I didn't know how evil he was. "Tell you what," I told him, "why don't you come over to my house Saturday morning and let's talk. I will play the priest and you can confess anything you want." He laughed and said, "Like hell!" But he showed and for over three hours he told me about himself. Some of it was very dark and painful, but he told it all. When he finished with his confession and a description of the pain he had experienced, I hugged him and we wept together. Over the years we walked together without masks.

Even though my friend lived in another city, we would occasionally see each other and we emailed often, as much as two or three times a week. When he "fell off the wagon" I was the only one he told; when he hurt someone and couldn't bear the fact that he had, he told me; when he was depressed and hated himself, I was the only one who knew. But there was more than that. We shared the laughter and joy of our lives too, and sometimes the successes. We could brag to each other . . . and you can only weep and brag before someone you trust. He knew my secrets and I knew his. Shortly before his death he had gotten a not-half-bad job in his profession, had bought an old secondhand car, and even had a small apartment.

Then he got plastered.

Then I got the message that he was dead.

There were those who saw my friend as a failure (he was that), an alcoholic (he was that), a horrible sinner (he was certainly that), and a not very pleasant human being (he was sometimes that too). But I knew him and when I heard that he was dead, I wept. I loved him and Jesus did too. Frankly I don't think I've ever known anyone who understood God's mercy, kindness, grace, and love more than my friend. It was often all he had and he clung to it with his entire being. I believe that however he died (and, as I said, I don't want to know), Jesus said to him, "Child, I know. It's enough. You come on Home."

I'm writing this book because I have a passion about God's people creating spaces where masks aren't necessary, where we can experience the freedom and joy of no longer being ashamed in the darkness behind our masks. Life is hard, our sins are great, and the wounds are deep. We simply can't do this thing without one another, and the loneliness is making us crazy.

But the truth is that we're not there yet. So if you decide to remove your mask, don't do it quickly. Before you remove your mask, make sure that the other person is someone who cares enough to listen to the reasons you wear the mask. If no one has that time or inclination, keep your mouth shut.

If you just read this chapter and understood it, I probably just saved your posterior.

Don't thank me. I was glad to do it.

Behind the Mask
1. Define "authenticity."
2. Describe "appropriate authenticity" and "inappropriate authenticity."

3. Why is a "safe place" important? What characterizes such a place?
4. How can we create a "safe place" for others and ourselves?

Background Scriptures: Matthew 7:6; Psalm 55:12–14; Proverbs 15:23.

Note to small group leaders: Refer to these Scriptures as needed during your discussion, along with Scripture passages in this chapter.

CHAPTER 3

I've Gotta Be Me

I do not understand my own actions. For I do not do what I want, but I do the very thing I hate. . . . For I know that nothing good dwells in me, that is, in my flesh. For I have the desire to do what is right, but not the ability to carry it out. For I do not do the good I want, but the evil I do not want is what I keep on doing. (Romans 7:15, 18–19)

I have a friend who told me that he was determined to take off his mask. "When I took it off," he said, "I found another mask." Then he said he took that one off and found yet another one. "I went through seven different masks and do you know what I found?"

I allowed I didn't.

"I found," he said, "that nothing was there."

I'm not suggesting that will happen to you. I am, however, suggesting that something far worse will happen when you start taking off the masks and looking at your real agendas. In fact, the process won't be very pretty. It involves a slow death and it's painful. The most dangerous prayer you can pray (if God deems to answer it) is, "God, show me myself."

Albert Camus was a twentieth-century French, Nobel Prize–winning, existentialist/absurdist author, philosopher, and atheist fascinated with the Christian faith. Camus's novel, *The Fall*, is about a man, Jean-Baptiste Clamence, and his encounter with the reality of who he really was. If you're familiar with the novel, you know that Clamence starts out as a respected Parisian lawyer who sees himself as selfless and kind. That mask is ripped off one evening while he walks home after being with his mistress. He encounters a woman getting ready to jump off a bridge to her death. Clamence notices her in passing . . . and then, when she jumps, he does nothing. He walks away with the sound of her screams in his ears.

That incident was a catalyst for an encounter with reality. The book is, in effect, a confessional. It is a series of monologues in an Amsterdam bar where Clamence stops hiding and ponders who he really is. If you read that novel and don't find yourself in it, put this book down because everything I say in this book in general—and in this chapter in particular—is going to irritate you beyond words.

One of the great fallacies of our time is the belief that we are all good people (with some rare exceptions) and if we can somehow fix the bad institutions, go to the right therapist, take the right medication, deal with the abuse we have encountered, get enough education, be trained properly, earn more money and the like, then that "good person" will emerge.

When Sammy Davis Jr. first sang the song, "I've Gotta Be Me," we all liked that he was willing to "go it alone" and that he couldn't "be right for somebody else if I'm not right for me." He had to be free. The assumption was that when he was free, he would be good.

Nice thought that. The problem is that it's simply not true.

I loved the late Brennan Manning and it's not because he was such a good person and Christian. I loved him because he wasn't . . . and, more important, he knew it. In the last book Manning wrote before his death, *All Is Grace*, the introduction was worth the price of the book. Here it is:

> *All Is Grace* was written in a certain frame of mind—
> that of a ragamuffin.
>
> Therefore,
> > This book is by the one who thought he'd
> > > be farther along by now, but he's not.
> > It is by the inmate who promised the parole
> > > board he'd be good, but he wasn't.
> > It is by the dim-eyed who showed the path
> > > to others but kept losing his way.
> > It is by the wet-brained who believed if a
> > > little wine is good for the stomach, then a lot
> > > is great.
> > It is by the liar, tramp, and thief; otherwise
> > > known as the priest, speaker, and author.
> > It is by the disciple whose cheese slid
> > > off his cracker so many times
> > > he said, "to hell with cheese 'n' crackers."
> But . . .

It is for those who strain at pious piffle
    because they've been swallowed by Mercy
    itself.
This book is for myself and those who have been
around
    the block enough times that we care to whisper
the ragamuffin's rumor—
    all is grace.[1]

The problem is that we can't get from here to there without revealing our hidden agendas and taking off our masks, if only to ourselves. If God should answer that dangerous prayer I mentioned ("God, show me myself"), and he usually does, what should you expect? There are a great variety of answers to that question because we're all wired differently and the masks we wear are often individualized. But there are also universals that we should expect and, if you don't encounter these universals, you're probably kidding yourself.

The Size of Our Ego

First, our ego is far bigger than we think it is and thus our motives are often a lot different from what we think they are.

I'm using "ego" in the popular sense of that word, meaning "self-centered." (The psychological definition, especially in psychoanalytical circles, refers to the part of one's mind that is the referee between what is conscious and unconscious, and accounts for a reality check. Counselors often refer to a "healthy ego," meaning good self-esteem.) Someone has described "religion" as what we do when nobody is looking. That definition is inadequate, but it is worth more than a passing thought.

While I have a natural aversion to any book with "purpose" or "driven" in the title, I think Rick Warren's book, *The Purpose Driven Life,* is wonderful. The most often quoted statement from that book is, "It's not about you,"[2] with the rest of the book pointing out that it really is about God. And while I liked the book, I'm going to scream (or cuss) the next time someone throws that quote at me. I'm a Calvinist and I know it's about God. In fact, I know it's *all* about God. He is the sovereign Creator, Ruler, and Sustainer of all that is. Okay? I get that.

The "It's not about you" is the hard part. The effort to make one's life, actions, and motivations about God will reveal a surprising discovery . . . and that discovery will not be very pretty. We discover that our motives are far more mixed and self-centered than we thought they were.

For instance, I'm a religious professional, and do lots and lots of religious stuff. Not only that, I get ego strokes from people about my doing religious stuff. People are always asking me to pray for them, answer questions about God, counsel them, correct some spurious theological assertion, love them, forgive them, help someone in need, or even adopt a stray cat they found. Because of my role as a religious professional, I fulfill those expectations reasonably well. The horror for me was the discovery that all of it was tainted with self-interest. I'm very concerned with what people will say about me and, when they say good things, I'm affirmed. Pretty soon I find myself playing a role that supports my belief that it's not about you . . . it's about me.

A while ago, Key Life did a live interview with Jared Wilson for our website and all the pastors on our mailing list. Jared was talking about his book *The Pastor's Justification.* If you're a pastor, you'll see yourself; if you're not a pastor, it will let you in on what is often true of pastors and, on reflection, true of you too. What Jared wrote is a series of questions designed to cause an honest pastor to wince; questions like:

- How many times have you boasted or gloried in numbers and dollars?
- How many times have you gloried in appearances and assumptions?
- How many times have you neglected orphans and widows?
- How many times have you daydreamed during a counseling session?
- How many times have you sacrificed your family on the altar of ministry, or your ministry on the altar of family?
- How many times have you listened to the same struggling church member recount the same sins over and over and wanted to just say, "Shut up, get a life, and leave me alone"?
- How many times have you seen the weekly pest approaching your office door and thought he wasn't worth your time?
- How many times have you bristled because you consider yourself above critique or challenge?
- How many times have you envied the pastor across the street for his skill in the pulpit or his way with people or his high attendance or big building or nicer car or better behaved children or hotter wife?
- How many times have you measured your church against another?
- How many times have you been disgruntled in your heart over your people for being too lazy or

too legalistically radical or too something else in between that makes you uncomfortable?
- How many times under stress and exhaustion have you peeked at pornography or lusted after a woman not your wife?
- How many times have you failed to confess your sins to another and be held accountable?
- How many times have you failed to seek help or seek sharpening or seek counseling?
- How many times have you chased countless poisonous idols of approval and validation?

Then Jared reminded his readers that someday we are going to stand before a holy God and the Bible teaches that pastors will be judged by a stricter standard. He asked what the pastor would think that holy God will say. His answer: "Justified!"[3]

Of course the "justified" part is the key and we'll talk a lot about that later. But for now, we need to understand the desperate need we all have for "justification." If it's about God and not about you, anything that isn't about God is about you. When I get "ego strokes" for doing all the religious "stuff," my actions cease to be all about God.

Jesus said that no human was good (Mark 10:18) because anything that is truly "good" must be for goodness' (i.e., God's) sake. When we bake cookies for our neighbor, visit a sick friend in the hospital, help out someone in need, or give money to the Salvation Army at Christmas, and the result is our feeling of satisfaction, righteousness, and purity, it ceases to be a purely good act.

But it gets worse.

The Success of Our Efforts

Second, not only are our motives far different from what we think, once we see the problem, the remedy is a lot harder than we ever supposed. So our efforts are far less successful than we had hoped. C. S. Lewis famously said that nobody knows how bad one is until one tries to be good. That's true, and it's one of the reasons Christians wear masks. I don't think I've ever met a Christian who didn't want to be better than he or she was, and therein lies the problem. If you're part of an organization (that would be the church) that is supposed to be marked by purity, goodness, and faithfulness, and you're having a hard time living up to that mark, you have to either leave or fake it, even sometimes fake it to yourself. That is the stuff of masks.

The standards are so high and there are so many of them! If you read the Bible much and don't feel horribly guilty and convicted, you're a fruitcake.

There's an old story about a lawyer who was in the hospital, having received the prognosis that he didn't have very long to live. When his pastor visited the lawyer, he found him frantically flipping through a Bible. "I never thought I would see you studying the Bible," the pastor commented. "I'm not," replied the lawyer. "I'm looking for loopholes."

There aren't any.

Just a cursory reading of the Ten Commandments, the Sermon on the Mount, or the lists of sins the apostle Paul had a tendency to declare should cause the most committed Christian to wince. I can hardly read a passage like Matthew 23 anymore. That's where Jesus says some very unpleasant things about the finest, most obedient, and thoroughly righteous people of his time. If you're a Christian, heavily involved in your church and doing the best you can, don't read Matthew 23 . . . especially at night if you want to get any sleep. It's not only that the anthropology of the Bible is quite negative (it is), it's the way the anthropological statements get "down and personal." It's not just that "the heart is deceitful above all things, and desperately sick; who can understand it?" (Jeremiah 17:9) or that "all have sinned and fall short of the glory of God" (Romans 3:23); it's the realization that *my* heart is deceitful above all things and *I* have sinned horribly and fall short of the glory of God.

As I move into the final years of my life, I'm quite disappointed that I'm not as good as I thought I would be by now. Don't get me wrong, I'm some better than I was but I'm not sure if that's Jesus or old age. I probably don't sin quite so much anymore but that's not because I don't want to. And therein is the reality of my life . . . struggle, failure, despair, and then Jesus.

I'm often accused of being "flippant about sin." I'm not. In fact, it's just the opposite. I know that obedience, purity, and holiness are the path of wholeness and peace. I know what would enable me to sleep better at night and reduce the shame, guilt, and fear I feel with the masks I wear. I know what I need to do. As in the Bob Newhart comedy sketch where he plays a psychiatrist, I need to "Stop it. Just stop it!" I know that turning away from my sin and walking the path of holiness would change everything for the better. I know what is required. In fact, you have never met a man who wants to please God more than I do, because I know what the Bible says. Thus, I know what God requires to get rid of the masks and to live free.

I've tried—really tried—to do what God requires. You don't know anybody who has tried more than I have. I'm ordained, for God's sake. I probably could have made more money and had a far easier life had I gone into vinyl repair. But I didn't. I followed God's call into ministry and, as far as I know (even though, looking back I see the masks and hidden agendas), I did it from a heart that wanted to please and glorify God and help his people. I knew (I'm not now nor was I then unaware of) my sins, my selfishness, and my rationalizations. But when I was young I knew that, while I needed a lot of work, there was time to get everything fixed. I'm not so young anymore and I'm shocked that so little has changed. In some ways, I've gotten worse. I've learned to hide it better, but at night when I finally drift off to sleep, I know.

There is an old story about the pastor who, when he was young, asked God to enable him to reach the world for Christ. When he was in his thirties, he asked God for the power to win his city to Christ. In his fifties, he changed his prayer to a request that he win his church to Christ. When he was close to retirement he prayed, "Lord, don't let me lose too many."

I understand that and, frankly, if you're over forty, you do too. The only reason I can write what I just wrote is that people are my business and I know that everything I said about myself is true of you too. At night, when there's nobody to impress, nobody to con, and nobody to lie to, you know the truth. That's the key to authenticity. If there are two kinds of people in the world—to wit, the good people and the bad people—then the bad people will have to wear masks in order to be accepted by the good people. But when one knows that there are two kinds of people in the world—the bad people who know it and the bad people who don't—then it's a whole new ballgame. It's a secret that makes removing the masks quite difficult and painful, but it is also a secret that makes removing them possible.

45

I remember how shocked I was when a respected deacon in the church I served came and confessed to me. Everybody thought he was godly and faithful, and with a powerful witness to Christ's work in his life. I've been a pastor for a long time and have heard more confessions than you would believe, far more than a district attorney in a Wall Street investigation, a Washington scandal, or a prostitution bust. So there isn't anything I haven't heard and I've grown weary of hearing twits tell me, "Reverend, someday I'm going to show you the 'real world.'" I see more of the "real world" in a week than most people see in a lifetime. If you've cleaned up as many suicides, buried as many babies, stood by as many deathbeds, and held as many sobbing people as I have, you've seen more of the real world than you ever thought you would see or want to see. So if you've listened to as many confessions as I have, you are pretty much unshockable.

But when this deacon came into my study and started weeping, I was close. Of all the people I knew, he was the last person I would ever think would steal money from his company. He told me that it was going to be in the papers the next day and he didn't want me to hear it from anybody but him. That night, as he gave me the details, he "came clean." We prayed together and I told him, "Bill, don't waste your sin." He asked me what I meant and I told him that we had a lot of new Christians in our church. His sin would be difficult for them to hear because so many looked up to him. "Bill, as I understand it, Jesus came to die for our sins because we needed it. Those new Christians need to know that Christians sin and they need to know how Christians deal with their sin."

He gave me permission to not only reveal his sin to our congregation but to use him as a model of how Christians take off their masks, stand naked before the world, and dance before the throne of a God who is never surprised and always kind.

I don't have the time or space to tell you the rest of the story, but it is wonderful. Our congregation surrounded my friend with love, went to his trial *en masse*, supported him and his family while he did jail time, and applauded when he was fully restored.

I'll never forget the rotunda of the courthouse where my friend was judged guilty and sentenced. There were others involved in the crime and one could hear their loud claims of innocence, feel their anger, and listen to their silly justifications. At the same time, brothers and sisters surrounded my friend (a kind of "holy huddle"). We were all praying for him, that God wouldn't waste his sin. In fact, my friend shined as he went off to jail, served his time, came home, and was restored fully by the congregation that loved him.

Those new Christians learned the truth about "how Christians do it." They will never forget. And a lot of other people who were not Christians won't forget either. They will always remember the broken sinner who had trouble getting his act together being loved and forgiven by other sinners who had trouble getting their acts together too.

The Holiness of Our God

But before we end this chapter, there is one more thing, and it's even worse than what I've written so far. Not only is our ego far bigger than we think and our efforts far less successful than we had hoped, third, we worship a God who is far more holy than we can possibly imagine.

Isaiah 6 is one of the most important chapters in the Bible. The prophet Isaiah was in the temple cleaning the candelabras and whistling an old Jewish song when the "real" God showed. It wasn't what Isaiah expected. The temple's foundations started shaking, there was smoke, and six large and terrifying winged creatures sang at the top of their lungs to the God whose robe filled the temple, "Holy, holy, holy is the LORD of hosts; the whole earth is full of his glory!" (Isaiah 6:3).

What do you think Isaiah did? Proclaim how hard he had tried? Do you think he listed the ways he had served God? How about putting on a smiley face (his mask) and kneeling quietly in prayer, thanking God for the "peace that passed understanding"? Are you crazy? Isaiah fell on his face, speechless before a holy and scary God. When he finally managed to say something, I suspect it came out as a croak: "Woe is me! For I am lost; for I am a man of unclean lips, and I dwell in the midst of a people of unclean lips; for my eyes have seen the King, the LORD of hosts!" (Isaiah 6:5).

That is the normal, expected, and sane reaction of someone who encounters a holy God. The reason for all the laws of the Bible, the lists of sins, and the calls for holiness and purity is not to make us better (at least not the main reason) but to bring us before the real God whose ways are not our ways and whose thoughts are not our thoughts (Isaiah 55:8), that we might take the first step to freedom. That first step is not getting better and better every day in every way, but looking at the absolutely overwhelming, frightening purity of the real God.

If you've read what I've written in this chapter and understood it, you have thereby affirmed a holy God. If you didn't, you did just the opposite. The better we think we are, the less we understand the holiness of God. Here's the principle: <u>Every time a believer starts feeling good about</u> <u>personal righteousness and purity, at that point God is</u> <u>brought down to the believer's level and becomes something</u> <u>less than the holy, righteous, and pure God of the Bible.</u>

But it's not just that the god we create is far different from the holy God of the Bible. The believer who raises himself to a level of goodness that satisfies that god and receives a pat on the back is not only living a lie, he is in a very dangerous place. "It is a fearful thing to fall into the hands of the living God" (Hebrews 10:31).

Rick Warren is right (even if it's irritating) when he says it's not about us, but God. It really is. We were created by God—a holy God—and, to play off Augustine's words, our hearts are phony, our lives dishonest, and our actions silly until they find some kind of rest in him. That "rest" is a lot different from what you think, but it starts by recognizing how dark the dark really is.

Now you're probably thinking, *Good heavens! You're a bundle of joy. Thanks a lot!*

Actually I just gave you a gift, even if it doesn't feel like it. For God's sake, don't waste your sin! It's a gift God gave you to set you free and it may be the most important gift (after Christ, of course) he's given to those he loves when those he loves are aware of it. And if you think of yourself as good, pure, and righteous, it's a curse for a lot of reasons, but the primary one is that it's simply not true. The principle is this: The quality of the prognosis is dependent upon the accuracy of the diagnosis. A physician who tells you that your cancer is a just a mild case of the flu may make you feel better, but that physician isn't doing you any favor.

With apologies to Emily Dickinson . . .

I'm screwed up! Who are you?
Are you screwed up, too?
Then there's a pair of us—don't tell!
They'd banish us, you know!

How dreary to pretend to be somebody!
How public like a frog
To tout your purity the lifelong day
To an admiring bog!

Behind the Mask

1. Why is it dangerous to pray, "God, show me myself"?
2. How are our motives mixed and self-centered?
3. What is the benefit of faking goodness and faithfulness?
4. How can you fool yourself?
5. How is being a "broken sinner" a good thing and a gift from God?
6. How can seeing the real God in his holiness be the first step to freedom?

Background Scriptures: Romans 7; Mark 10:18; Jeremiah 17:9; Matthew 23; Isaiah 6; Romans 3:23

Note to small group leaders: Refer to these Scriptures as needed during your discussion, along with Scripture passages in this chapter.

CHAPTER 4

The Devil's Trinity

There is no fear in love, but perfect love casts out fear. For fear has to do with punishment, and whoever fears has not been perfected in love. We love because he first loved us. (1 John 4:18–19)

Did you hear about the man who decided to commit suicide and decided to do it right? He got a can of gasoline, a rope, a bottle of poison, a gun, and a boat. He rowed out in a lake under an overhanging tree. He threw the rope over a limb and put it around his neck, doused himself with gasoline, drank the poison, struck a match, and put the gun to his head and pulled the trigger. He missed his head and instead hit the rope, cutting it in two. The match started a fire but he fell off the boat, putting it out. Then he became so nauseous he gagged and spit up the poison. "If I had not been a good swimmer," he said later, "I could have died."

There is something like that about the Devil's trinity of shame, guilt, and fear—what is very bad can be the key to what is very good. Fear shows our helplessness, shame defines our problem, and guilt drives us to God. The Devil's most effective tools become, as it were, the keys to health and wholeness. Masks are made from the material of shame, guilt, and fear, but it is also the manure in which God grows flowers. Just as Solzhenitsyn blessed the prison in which he suffered and the rotting straw on which he slept,[1] wise Christians have learned to bless the curse of shame, guilt, and fear.

But I'm getting ahead of myself.

Not too long ago I talked to a good friend who went through one of the most horrifying experiences we can face. We talked, prayed, and wept together. His sin (and it was bad) was publicly revealed and his church required him to confess it before the entire church (a practice with which I have some serious problems). We all have secrets that shame us and create guilt. And we all live, to one degree or another, in fear that others will find out. The thought of public revelation is almost overwhelming.

My friend's worst nightmare became the reality and it almost killed him.

That's bad. Yeah, it was, but God grew a flower in that horrible soil. Let me give you part of what my friend wrote to his church:

Every part of me wants to flee this town and never have to look anyone in the face again. I've begged God to let me go, but I'm still here. This morning I woke thinking of the parallels in my life and my father's life and what is happening now. I am in the middle of a scandal in the same town he was over thirty years ago. I always swore I'd never be as stupid as he was, yet here I am. I'm faced with choices: I could blame others as my father did and die a slow, miserable death, being eaten away with the acid of bitterness. I could commit suicide, leaving my family with nothing. Or I could give it—my shame, my fear, and my guilt—to the only One who can carry it.

[All his life, my friend had worn a mask that hid who he really was. On the outside, the mask was pretty, clean, and religious. He said that he once spilled a bucket of paint in the garage and that his father was livid. He said that he had been working hard not to spill paint all his life . . .]

I'm so very tired of doing it. As a matter of fact, I can't anymore. The words "I am sorry" seem too shallow, and I'm very sorry for not loving all of you. There is no excuse, but there is relief. Jesus said, "It is finished." I'm here because I believe that. In this knowledge I am breaking the generational chains that have held me captive my entire life. I'm finally loved.

Frankly, my friend paid a big price—one you and I both hope we never have to pay—but he is now free and, with the emancipated slave, can shout, "Free at last! Free at last! Thank God Almighty, I'm free at last!"

Years ago I interviewed Jim Bakker, the disgraced founder of the PTL Club, after he got out of prison. I asked him how his experience of being convicted, publicly shamed, and going to prison affected him. "The most important thing," he said, "is that I'm free. Before I had to be so very careful and protect my image. Now I can go anywhere, be with anyone, and say anything, and it's pretty 'heady.'"

I know of no better place to start this discussion of fear, shame, and guilt than with the words and definitions from

Edward T. Welch's very good book, *Shame Interrupted: How God Lifts the Pain of Worthlessness and Rejection.*

> Shame and guilt are close companions but not identical. Shame is the more common and broader of the two. In Scripture you will find shame (nakedness, dishonor, disgrace, defilement) about ten times more often than you find guilt.
>
> Guilt lives in the courtroom where you stand alone before the judge. It says, "You are responsible for wrongdoing and legally answerable." "You are wrong." "You have sinned." The guilty person expects punishment and needs forgiveness.
>
> Shame lives in the community, though the community can feel like a courtroom. It says, "You don't belong—you are unacceptable, unclean, and disgraced" because "You are wrong, you have sinned" (guilt), *or* "Wrong has been done to you" *or* "You are associated with those who are disgraced or outcast." The shamed person feels worthless, expects rejection, and needs cleansing, fellowship, love, and acceptance.[2]

In what follows we're going to spend some time getting to know the members of the Devil's trinity by paying a visit to the community, the courtroom, and the prison, but first I want to give you the key to killing off that dark trinity.

> Jesus loves me! This I know,
> For the Bible tells me so;
> Little ones to Him belong;
> They are weak, but He is strong.

Yes, Jesus loves me!
Yes, Jesus loves me!
Yes, Jesus loves me!
The Bible tells me so.

We'll get to that in the next chapter, but now I want to visit . . .

The Community

I'm a loner. In fact, if they would let me bring my wife, I would go and live in a monastery. I often teach seminary students the importance of having a ministry philosophy. They need a basic philosophy that defines who they are, what God has called them to do, and how they propose to go about doing it. As a pastor, I used to kid the congregation, "Here's my ministry philosophy: I'll leave you alone if you leave me alone." The congregation would laugh because they thought it was a joke. I would often say to those people, "Look, I'm not your mother." The reason I said that is because that's exactly what was happening. I was becoming their mother, staying up at night, worried about them; trying to fix them; and being overly directive.

I remember an incident that happened after our church's regular Wednesday evening service. Generally I would teach and then head for my study, locking the door and remaining there until all the people left. Then I would go out to the parking lot, get in my car, and drive home. On this occasion, I got caught. There was a woman standing in the parking lot talking to a young man. When she saw me, she came over to my car and said, "Steve, I've been talking to this guy who came to our church tonight for the first time." I told her that I was glad he had come, but before I could get my car moving, she continued, "But there's a problem. He said that nobody spoke to him . . . not one single person. I told him that we don't come here to be loved. We come here to be taught. That's right, isn't it?"

I don't remember what I said to her but I remember what I thought driving home—something was seriously wrong with me, the church, and what I had been teaching and demonstrating to my congregation. After a sleepless night and a good deal of prayer and confession, God started doing something to me for which I don't think I've ever forgiven him. For my sake and their sake, he put people on my heart. William Booth, founder of The Salvation Army, is said to have answered a question about his success this way: "From the day I got the poor of London on my heart . . . God had all of William Booth there was."

That sounds good and godly but—trust me on this—it isn't a gift unmixed with some really bad, messy, and crazy stuff. Someone described the church as a bunch of porcupines huddling together in a storm. It is that . . . and so is the community where you live, move, and have your being. It doesn't matter if it's your school, business, golf or poker buddies, book club, neighborhood or alumni association— dealing with people is not for sissies. But you need people, and that is both a blessing and a curse.

God didn't create us to exist in a vacuum. He called us to community. It isn't good for man/woman to be alone (Genesis 2:18). The psalmist wrote, "Behold, how good and pleasant it is when brothers dwell in unity!" (Psalm 133:1). Most Christians know that and talk about it. "Community" is a sort of "in" topic in religious circles. The problem is that it sounds a lot easier than it is.

I will often say to churches where I preach or speak, "If you're visiting today, we're so glad you're here, but let me give you some advice from the old guy. Leave before you get hurt. We are not nice people. We have a tendency to gather in cliques and it's hard to break into them. We are not models of civility and kindness. Sometimes we'll talk about you behind your back. We yell at each other a lot and the communication is sometimes so bad that we don't have the foggiest what the other person is saying, feeling, or thinking. We aren't what we appear and you shouldn't let the Bibles fool you. So, leave before you get hurt." (Just so you know, I also say, "But if you manage to get over all of that and stay, you'll find a family here, and we'll love each other. It may be the most significant family you'll ever experience. In fact, it could change your life.")

That brings up a question. If we were created by God to be in community, if we need to be with other people and they need to be with us, and if God works in and through his family, why is it so hard? If the song is right and "people who need people are the luckiest people in the world," why is it so painful? If we are created for intimacy with others, why is there so little of it?

It's the shame, dummy.

You scare the spit out of me. I'm worried that you will see what's behind the mask and reject me. There are things in my life that would surprise and offend you. I have secrets that I've shared with no one but God, and I certainly can't share them with you because you'll be shocked and offended. Then you will have nothing more to do with me . . . and I need you.

Don't ever underestimate the power of shame in the lives of everybody you know and in you. It's the reason we wear masks. Just about every week we hear of the tragic result of public shame in social media—depression, suicides, and emotional breakdowns. My emotional health and well-being are inexorably connected to you and to what you think of me. It keeps me awake at night, it causes great fear, it draws me to you, and then it makes me want to run.

The problem is that people really do need people. We are created that way. And the "hell" of it is that the very thing we desire is the very thing that prevents us from having it. I yearn to love and be loved, to accept and be accepted, to affirm and be affirmed, but my mask won't let me.

One often hears from adults that teenagers should be grateful for their youth and teen years because "those are the happiest times in your life." That's insane. My teen years were the most miserable of my entire life. I wasn't old enough to have learned to create masks sophisticated enough to fool everyone. I don't ever want to go back to those years. I was always on the "outside" trying to get to the "inside." I never felt good enough or "cool" enough to be accepted and affirmed by others. And the horror of it all was that I couldn't hide it. When parents say they don't understand their teenage kids—the anger, sullenness, withdrawal, mood swings, and rebellion—it is because those kids don't understand themselves and don't know how to fix it.

As we grow older it gets better, but the "better" doesn't have to do with self-acceptance or comfort with others. It has to do with the ability to fake it better than we did when we were teenagers. One of my friends says that Christians appear to be better than others because Christians know the rules and can fake it better than others can. That's true of most adults and masks. It isn't that we don't wear masks; it's just that we have learned the rules and create better masks than teenagers do.

Let me give you a profound quote from C. S. Lewis:

> Every man, not very bold or very arrogant, has to "live up to" the outward appearance of other men: he knows there is that within him which falls far below even his most careless public behavior. . . . We have never told the whole truth. We may confess ugly *facts*—the meanest cowardice or the shabbiest and most prosaic impurity—but the *tone* is false. The very act of confessing—an infinitesimally hypocritical glance—a dash of humor—all this contrives to dissociate the facts from your very self. . . . But the important thing is that we should not mistake our inevitably limited utterance for a full account of the worst that is inside.[3]

Our shame makes our community into a play where the actors play parts to please the audience. And when the play is over, everybody goes home to the same loneliness, emptiness, and shame . . . bundles of need with nothing but the pain.

Are there reasons for shame? Of course there are. The Scriptures are replete with images and admonitions of how we should live. In that sense, there are legitimate reasons for shame. However—and this is important—the Scriptures are also replete with illustrations of those who didn't live that way. And the most important thing is that those illustrations are very often the heroes of our faith. Flipping through the Bible should give all of us an attack of sanity. You can read about how it all got started when Jacob stole his birthright, Abraham's lying about his wife and saying she was his sister so she could enter the king's harem, Tamar's seductive ways, David's adultery and murder, Jeremiah's fear, Paul and Barnabas's anger and jealousy, Mark's cowardice, Peter's hypocrisy . . . and it goes on and on.

Do you think God is up to something? He is, but we must move on to . . .

The Courtroom

A lawyer friend recently got in an automobile accident. He backed up and hit a van while he and the van driver were waiting at a stoplight. It was clearly my friend's fault and he got the citation. Later he told me that it would never go on his record, he would never have to pay the $250 fine, he would never be found guilty, and he would never have to go to traffic school or get points on his license. I told him that I knew he was a gifted lawyer, but no lawyer was that good. "You don't understand," my friend said, "I asked for a trial in traffic court. In order for me to be found guilty, the police officer will have to come and witness against me. He has so much to do that he'll never show. The van driver knows that the damage to his van was minor, and he has a day job and won't show either. So without witnesses, the citation will be dismissed."

That's what happened in John 8 with the woman caught in adultery. There weren't any accusers. Jesus wrote something in the sand and said, "Let him who is without sin among you be the first to throw a stone at her" (John 8:7). Nobody did. Instead they disappeared—heels and elbows flying as they ran away. Then Jesus asked the woman, "Woman, where are they? Has no one condemned you?" (John 8:10). There weren't any accusers.

The woman did commit the sin (and a horrible one, at that) of adultery. It is, after all, one of the "Big Ten." I know, I know, it makes me angry too that the man she had slept with wasn't being accused. Nevertheless, I'm glad there weren't any accusers and that Jesus didn't condemn her.

Still, she sinned.

If you read the last chapter, you know that the Bible isn't very positive about human nature. Biblical anthropology is quite negative. Nothing I say here should detract from what God says about sin and our failure in fixing the problem. It is serious business. Christians are called to be holy and God is never reticent about giving specifics concerning what that means. When Jonathan Edwards preached his sermon, "Sinners in the Hands of an Angry God," it was scary. What Edwards said was true.

(As an aside, Jonathan Edwards has gotten a "bum rap" in American culture. For years, because that sermon was included in every American literature anthology, it was all most Americans knew about Edwards. That's sad because there was so much more to him than that sermon and even that sermon didn't represent the major thrust of his preaching. He was the first president of Princeton and perhaps the finest philosophical mind America ever created. But I digress.)

We are sinners and there really are accusers. They're everywhere (file that under shame), and the sad part is that those accusers are right. "Bless those who curse you," someone said. "Think what they would say if they knew the truth." Not only that, the law of God—a holy and righteous God—accuses us. And for the purposes of this book, we accuse ourselves. We know. No matter how much we protest, listen to drivel from therapists about false guilt, and have friends who affirm our goodness, we're still guilty. The psychiatrist who said to her client, "The reason you have an inferiority complex is that you are inferior," wasn't very helpful. However, if she had said to the client, "The reason you feel guilty is because you are guilty," she would have been right on.

Sin isn't sin because it's "nasty" and simply "not done" by proper Christians. Sin is sin because it is destructive, vicious, and dangerous. Sin destroys all that is honorable, just, pure, lovely, and commendable (Philippians 4:8). It destroys relationships and families. It makes us hollow and empty, and it pokes at us every time we try to sleep or rest. Sometimes booze, a movie, or a church service will help for a while, but we still know and, in that knowing, we are without hope.

My friend Paul Tripp calls the place we live "the costume kingdom." He writes, "As a sinner, I am still seeking to be the king of a costume kingdom. You see, the problem with the little kingdom (the civilization of self) is that it dresses up and puts on the mask of things that are righteous and good, while it is capturing the heart for the glory of self. The most dangerous kinds of self-focus are those that take on the form of the good things of the Kingdom of God."[4]

There are those, of course, who lower the standard. But that doesn't work in a courtroom. There is something inflexible about the law. If you read the Sermon on the Mount (preached by Jesus and found in Matthew 5—7) you know that Jesus didn't just proclaim the law of God; he ratcheted it up just so we would know what was behind God's holiness and his law. For instance, Jesus said that a lustful thought was as wrong and sinful as an adulterous act, that being angry with someone was as bad as killing them, and that we weren't only called to love our family and friends but we were called to love and pray for our enemies. Jesus was telling us two things that are very important. The first is the blinding and disturbing holiness of a holy God. The second is that Jesus was bringing us to the realization of "None is righteous, no, not one" (Romans 3:10).

A number of years ago a friend (and a religious leader) had been sleeping with the wife of another man. When the husband found out, he publicly accused my friend. Then my friend tried to hire someone to kill the husband. The person he tried to hire turned out to be an undercover police officer. (I know, I know. I don't run in very good company.) I remember how I felt the next day, when the front pages of the local newspapers detailed what he had done. The headlines leapt off the page and I winced.

The next day my friend called me and said that he supposed I had read the papers. I allowed that I had. "Steve," he said, "I'm innocent. I need you to stand with me at my trial."

I replied, "Innocent? Are you crazy? You're guilty as sin and you're not only guilty of the accusations, you're guilty of stupidity . . . and stupid is forever." I told my friend that I would go with him to his trial (which I did) but that I wouldn't say he was innocent to anybody. He wasn't innocent, and he went to prison because the law judged him accurately. Sometimes that happens in our human courts and sometimes it doesn't, but in God's courtroom the judgment is always accurate. There is no wiggle room. Every lie, every bit of jealousy and envy, every root of bitterness, every time you lusted, every time you demeaned others, every time you failed to feed the poor, and every time you expressed a racist comment, all of that will be exposed and you will be found guilty.

If that doesn't scare the spit out of you, you're crazy.

Not only should that scare the spit out of you, it will lead you to . . .

The Prison

In Romans 7, the apostle Paul confesses his sins. It's something no religious leader should do if he or she wants to keep his or her job. Paul's honesty is quite astonishing. Before that, he said Christ came to save sinners and he was "the worst" (1 Timothy 1:15 NIV). It's one thing to say it and it's quite another to give details. In that surprising confession of Paul in Romans, he cries out in the end, "Wretched man that I am! Who will deliver me from this body of death?" (Romans 7: 24).

Yeah, you're thinking, that's really bad. It is. Our masks are killing our relationships because relationships won't work without a modicum of authenticity and we simply can't risk it. And if that weren't bad enough, the God we would go to for comfort isn't any safer than the people we would like to go to for comfort. In fact, it's even worse, because God's holiness is a "consuming fire." Once one understands those hard truths, we just get more committed to hiding behind our masks and promoting our hidden agendas. The spiral goes deeper and the darkness grows darker.

I have a friend who wrote me not too long ago about the "pictures" she had spent her life trying to draw. "Seems the higher I dreamed, the harder I would fall," she wrote. "I always felt everyone wanted me to draw something other than what I wanted to draw. So, wanting to please and be loved, I would try to draw a picture they would like. But I don't think it really mattered what picture I would draw. It was never good enough and it was never appreciated. I guess what I was wanting was to make them happy, and I have lived long enough to realize that I could never and will never draw that picture." Her pictures didn't please the people she loved and God was holy. Better stop trying to draw pictures. Good thought that . . . and the beginning of wisdom.

I know these last two chapters have been dark and depressing. I promise it will get better but, lest I leave on a negative note, let me end this chapter where I started, with 1 John 4:18–19. Read it and then we'll talk about it: "There is no fear in love, but perfect love casts out fear. For fear has to do with punishment, and whoever fears has not been perfected in love. We love because he first loved us."

Behind the Mask

1. What is your personal struggle with shame, guilt, and fear?
2. How can shame, guilt, and fear be good things?
3. How are you at/with community?
4. How is sin "destructive, vicious, and dangerous"? Give examples.
5. What is the ultimate solution to our sin—including the shame, guilt, and fear that result—and our masks?

Background Scriptures: 1 John 4:18–19; Genesis 2:18; Psalm 133:1; Philippians 4:8; Matthew 5—7; Romans 3:10; Romans 7

Note to small group leaders: Refer to these Scriptures as needed during your discussion, along with Scripture passages in this chapter.

CHAPTER 5

Names for the Nameless

"I will give him a white stone, with a new name written on the stone that no one knows except the one who receives it." (Revelation 2:17)

While I was working on this chapter, I got a call from a man who wouldn't give his name. My assistant buzzed me, laughing. "I have a man on the line who says he needs to talk with you and that it's urgent," she said. "He says that he's a big fan of yours. By the way, he's lying about that. He called you 'Dr. Greene.'"

When I picked up the phone and said hello, I asked the man his name. "Let's go with Bobby," he said, "if that's okay with you. I don't want to give you my real name because I'm ashamed about what I'm going to tell you and, after I tell you, you won't want to have anything to do with me. I would rather you not know who I am."

It was an interesting conversation because neither of us knew the other's name.

We don't, you know. Know each other's names, that is.

In the Bible, names aren't just names. The name reveals the essence of the person. In fact, sometimes the names of biblical figures were changed to reflect a change in who they were. Revelation 2:17 says that we'll have a new name in heaven and that name will reflect who we really, ultimately, are. My pointing that out probably makes both of us uncomfortable. If our name reflects the essence of who we are, then everybody will know, and (we assume) that "name" won't be very appealing.

Isaiah, the prophet, had some good news for God's people: "Say to the daughter of Zion, 'Behold, your salvation comes; behold, his reward is with him, and his recompense before him.' And they shall be called The Holy People, The Redeemed of the LORD; and you shall be called Sought Out, A City Not Forsaken" (Isaiah 62:11–12).

I have some good news for you too! It's about your name, and it's not what you think.

It is said that Augustine, after he had committed his life to Christ, was approached by his former mistress. When he saw her, he started running in the other direction. She ran after him shouting, "Augustine, it's me! It's me!" "Yes," he called back over his shoulder, "but it's not me!"

When Augustine said, "But it's not me!" it really *wasn't* him! And therein lies the best news you'll ever hear.

Let's start with a statement made by the apostle Paul in Galatians 2:19–20: "For through the law I died to the law, so that I might live to God. I have been crucified with Christ. It is no longer I who live, but Christ who lives in me. And the life I now live in the flesh I live by faith in the Son of God, who loved me and gave himself for me."

According to Paul, the good news is that you're already dead (we'll talk a lot more about that in the next chapter).

Normally, I know that isn't good news, but it is in this case, and I'm going to show you why. Please note that in the verses I gave you, Paul isn't giving us a command. He's giving us a fact. It isn't one more thing you have to do (crucify yourself) to "get right with God," "to change the world" or "to make your life count." The truth is that it's already done. When Jesus said, "It is finished," it really was finished . . . done . . . over. In Romans 6:11, Paul wrote that we should "consider [i.e., reckon, number, think of yourself] yourselves dead to sin and alive to God in Christ Jesus." In other words, we should think in a new way about who we really are.

When you die, you not only experience resurrection, you get a new name. The name is Forgiven, Redeemed, Acceptable, and Loved. That changes everything about our hidden agendas and our masks. When you're crucified with Christ . . .

Your Name Is Forgiven

I once asked a Jewish friend to forgive the church and me for what we did to Jews in the name of Christ. I waited for him to tell me to get lost or, maybe, to forgive me. Instead, he started weeping. I had no idea why and asked him. "Steve," he said, "I didn't hear a 'kicker' in your remarks. Often people will say something like what you said to me but there is always a kicker. You guys want me to receive Jesus, get saved, or to ask for forgiveness for what 'we' did to Jesus. I waited for the kicker and there wasn't one. Thank you."

That conversation is one I've thought about a lot. One of the most tragic things about the church is that we have become, as it were, a "church of kickers." It's the "Of course God loves you . . . but don't let it go to your head," "God will forgive you . . . but don't do it again," "God's your loving Father. . . but don't forget about the discipline," or "God loves you . . . but that should make a better person." I can't tell you the number of times I've brought up Jesus and the woman caught in adultery, his love and forgiveness given to her (John 8:1–11), and people will bring in the kicker: "Yeah, but don't forget that Jesus told her to 'sin no more.'" It's not that there isn't some truth in those statements. But they sometimes make God's love and forgiveness so conditional that, frankly, I can't deal with it. What was meant as good news very quickly becomes bad news because of the kicker.

I have an acquaintance in the billboard business. During the "troubles" in Northern Ireland he wanted to do something about the hatred between Catholics and Protestants. Do you know what he did? He bought billboards across Northern Ireland with one message: "I love you! Is that okay?—Jesus." That was a powerful message and it wasn't powerful because Jesus said that he loved them. Everybody knows that. It was powerful because there wasn't a kicker.

You're forgiven.

I know, I know. Your "Pavlovian" response (and mine) is to wait for the kicker. You can keep on waiting because there isn't one. It doesn't matter where you've been, who you're sleeping with, what you're drinking or smoking, what you think, who you've hurt, the games you're playing, the masks you're wearing, the agendas you're hiding, or whether or not you get better. When you bring it all to Jesus, you're forgiven.

Deal with it.

As an aside, the fact that our new name is Forgiven has amazing implications for relationships between Christians and for the masks we wear. The reason Jesus embedded "Forgive us our debts as we forgive those who have sinned against us" in the prayer he taught us is that he knew that without forgiveness at the heart of our relationships, we would continue to play at religion, and never love or be loved.

You can't forgive until you have been unconditionally forgiven (no kicker) and then you can only love to the degree to which you have been unconditionally forgiven. I will never remove my mask and set aside my agendas as long as I think Christianity is about fixing me and others, building empires, changing the world, making my life count, correcting doctrinal truth, promoting programs, raising money, and being nice. It's not. It's about the forgiveness of sins. Paul wrote, "The saying is trustworthy and deserving of full acceptance, that Christ Jesus came into the world to save sinners, of whom I am the foremost" (1 Timothy 1:15). Paul, your name is "Forgiven."

If you know Jesus, yours is too.

Are there implications to that? Of course there are . . . sometimes. Does it make you a better person? Of course it does . . . sometimes. Does it make a difference in your relationships? Of course it does . . . sometimes. Does it bring you into the stream of compassion and practical ministry to the world? Of course it does . . . sometimes. Does it give you a "burden for souls"? Of course it does . . . sometimes. And sometimes it doesn't. That's not the issue. Your name is "Forgiven." Rejoice and be glad.

But you have other names too. When you're crucified with Christ . . .

Your Name Is Redeemed

The word "redeemed" is a very strong word. It means to gain or regain something at a price. The Scripture says that in Christ we have been redeemed "through his blood, the forgiveness of our trespasses, according to the riches of his grace, which he lavished upon us" (Ephesians 1:7–8). Again, "For all have sinned and fall short of the glory of God, and are justified by his grace as a gift, through the redemption that is in Christ Jesus" (Romans 3:23–24).

There is an old sermon illustration about a boy who worked hours making a small boat. He took it down to the seashore and put it in the water. To his horror, the boat was picked up by a wave and carried out into the ocean, eventually disappearing. It was sad because he had worked so hard and long making the boat. Later he was walking by a pawnshop and saw his lost boat in the shop window. He told the pawnbroker that it was his boat but the pawnbroker said, "It may have been yours, but it's mine now. If you want it back, you'll have to pay for it like anybody else."

The boy worked all summer. He mowed lawns, babysat, and walked dogs to get enough money to buy back his boat. When he had enough, the boy went back to the pawnshop and purchased it. As he walked out of the shop he was heard to say, looking at his boat, "Little boat, I made you, I lost you, I found you, I bought you back, and now you're mine, all mine."

That's what happened to us. God said, "I made you, I lost you, I found you, I bought you back, and now you're mine." But being his isn't just about ownership; it's about being adopted by a father who is rich, generous, and kind. The Bible says that he "has delivered us from the domain of darkness and transferred us to the kingdom of his beloved Son, in whom we have redemption . . ." (Colossians 1:13–14). Again, the Scripture says that God has sent the Spirit of Jesus into our hearts, causing us to cry out, "Abba Father." "So you are no longer a slave, but a son, and if a son, then an heir through God" (Galatians 4:6–7).

I'm often asked what I do. I never know exactly what to say. Sometimes I say that I'm a preacher, or clergyman, or pastor, or professor, or writer, or broadcaster. There are times when I say that I'm a "religious professional" who "works for God." A friend of mine told me to stop saying that: "When you work for someone, you have a job as long as there is work to do and you do it well enough to please the boss. But when the day's work is over, you leave and go back to the house you paid for with the money you earned. Steve, you don't work for God. You're his son. When the day is over, you go up to the big house where you live. Try to remember that."

I do. My name is "Redeemed." That's your name too.

But you have other names as well, because when you're crucified with Christ . . .

Your Name Is Acceptable

Most Christians have a handle on the forgiveness thing. You're forgiven and then you work hard to be good. It's all about pleasing God, being faithful, and trying your best to be obedient. It's hard but we love to quote that "in Christ we can do all things." In other words, a Christian is forgiven and then he or she becomes better and better every day in every way.

What if I told you that God was already pleased, that he already thinks of you as faithful, and in his eyes you are already obedient? It's true. The theological word is "imputation" and it is so radical, so amazing, and so unbelievable that I have trouble believing it. But God said it and, unless he's started lying, it's true.

The Bible says, ". . . and be found in him, not having a righteousness of my own that comes from the law, but that which comes through faith in Christ . . ." (Philippians 3:9).

"Abraham believed God, and it was counted to him as righteousness" (Romans 4:3). "For Christ is the end of the law for righteousness to everyone who believes" (Romans 10:4). "And to the one who does not work but believes in him who justifies the ungodly, his faith is counted as righteousness" (Romans 4:5). "I will greatly rejoice in the LORD; my soul shall exult in my God, for he has clothed me with the garments of salvation; he has covered me with the robe of righteousness . . ." (Isaiah 61:10).

When Christ died on the cross, there was a trade. God traded my sin for Christ's righteousness. I would have settled for forgiveness because that is more than I deserve. The problem with forgiveness is that it can become something similar to a professor who cuts slack for a student. "Okay," the professor says, "I'm going to overlook your poor work and give you a passing grade, but don't ask me to continue doing this for you. You are going to have to work harder." Imputation is far more than that. It's the trade whereby the professor's academic record becomes yours.

I went to a banquet once where ties were required. Nobody had told me. A friend of mine saw me outside the banquet hall and said, "Steve, you don't have a tie. I have an extra one in my room. I'll be right back." Two minutes later he handed me a tie. I put it on and was acceptable.

The interesting thing about the tie my friend gave me is that it was his best tie. All evening people said to me, "Nice tie!" Not only was I dressed properly with a tie, I was dressed extravagantly with the best tie in the house.

That's what God has done to make us "Acceptable." He's given us the best clothes in the house, the righteousness of Christ.

In John Bunyan's *Pilgrim's Progress,* Mercy, one of the characters traveling with Christiana, Christian's wife, laughs in her sleep. Christiana asks Mercy about it and Mercy explains that she had a dream in which she was very convicted about her "hardness of heart." Then, in her dream, Mercy says a man came and wiped her tears with his handkerchief and dressed her in silver and gold—clothed, as it were, in the righteousness of Christ. Then he takes her to the throne room of a holy God where Mercy hears, "Welcome, daughter!"

That was my experience.

You see, as my friend Rod Rosenbladt, says, "It's not what's in your heart, it's about what is in God's heart."[1] They told me that God was holy. He is. They said that he was a consuming fire. He is. They told me that if I worked at it, studied "to show myself approved," and if I were faithful and obedient, the holy God would be pleased. They were right. But I just couldn't do it. Don't get me wrong, I tried. I really tried hard. My heart and my "clothes" were simply too dirty to get clean. Finally, I gave up and started to walk away.

That's when I looked down at my new clothes—the righteousness of Christ—and I heard his voice, "Welcome, child! Welcome!"

I laughed too.

But there's one more name. When you're crucified with Christ . . .

Your Name Is Loved

You should meet my wife Anna. She's a saint. Very few could live with somebody like me. And just so you know, I'm not being "authentic" or "humble" when I say that. It's the truth. I can be angry and kind in the same sentence, happy and sad in the same hour, and loving and hateful in the same day. I would be bipolar if either my manic state or my depressive state lasted longer. Anna, on the other hand, is the same yesterday, today, and forever. She is a gift from God and an anchor for this crusty old preacher.

I don't want to get too detailed here (you're not that safe) but the other day I called home and my wife wasn't there. I left a message on our answering machine. I don't even remember what the message was but I'm almost positive that it included the words, "Love you." I happened to get home before my wife did and listened to the message I'd left. I was shocked. I sounded ticked, upset, and kind of harsh. When I got home, I told Anna that I had listened to my message (the one intended for her). "I sounded very angry in that message . . . and I was wondering if I always sound like that." She smiled and I knew. "I'm so sorry," I told her. "I'm going to be a lot kinder than I have been." She smiled again and then . . .

. . . she gave me a Baby Ruth.

A Baby Ruth?

Yeah, and she's been doing that for almost all of our adult life. In fact, sometimes I fake bad stuff when I'm hungry, just to get a Baby Ruth. When I yell, forget a birthday or anniversary, do something a preacher ought not do, I get a Baby Ruth. Of course I don't deserve the Baby Ruth. That's the point of love. The principle is this: you can't experience love until it's given when you don't deserve it. Everything else is reward.

That's what God has done. Listen to what Paul writes: "For I am sure that neither death nor life, nor angels nor rulers, nor things present nor things to come, nor powers, nor height nor depth, nor anything else in all creation, will be able to separate us from the love of God in Christ Jesus our Lord" (Romans 8:38–39). I would suggest that those words pretty much cover it. They cover all of our masks and all of our hidden agendas.

God gives out Baby Ruths! Bet nobody ever told you that before.

Now turn the page and we'll talk about death. Don't worry. It's not what you think.

Behind the Mask

1. You're forgiven without a kicker. Sit with that a moment. What does that mean to/for you? What does God's forgiveness do to your masks and agendas?

2. As a son or daughter, you are "adopted by a father who is rich, generous, and kind." Do you really believe that? How would you live if you did?

3. "It's all about pleasing God, being faithful, and trying your best to be obedient." Why doesn't this work? What is it about instead?

4. How does God's unconditional love cover all your masks and hidden agendas?

Background Scriptures: Revelation 2:17; Galatians 2:19–20; Galatians 4:6–7; Colossians 1:13–14; Philippians 3:9; Romans 8

Note to small group leaders: Refer to these Scriptures as needed during your discussion, along with Scripture passages in the chapter.

CHAPTER 6

Dead Men (and Women) Do Tell Tales

For the death he died he died to sin, once for all, but the life he lives he lives to God. So you also must consider yourselves dead to sin and alive to God in Christ Jesus. (Romans 6:10–11)

Did you hear about the man in the hospital for emotional problems? He thought he was dead. They tried everything. Freud didn't work, medication didn't work, and diet didn't help. The man was sure he was dead and nobody could convince him otherwise.

Finally, one of the psychiatrists got a bright idea. It wasn't necessarily good psychology; but then, when that doesn't work, common sense might. The psychiatrist went to the man and said, "Sam, do dead men bleed?"

"Of course not," said Sam.

"Are you sure?"

"Of course, I'm sure. Everybody knows that dead men don't bleed."

That's when the psychiatrist pulled out a safety pin, opened it, and stuck Sam in the hand. He began to bleed. The psychiatrist thought he had finally fixed the problem until Sam looked at his hand. "Son of a gun," he said incredulously, "dead men do bleed!"

Sorry.

I got an email this morning from a man who was devastated. He understands grace and he knows that when Christ died, he died for all his sins—past, present, and future—but he said that recently someone he loved said, "Yes, God will always love you but your sin breaks his heart." I don't know who that "someone" was, but I hope it wasn't his mother. I said some rather unkind things about how he had been manipulated and about the "Pharisee" who had manipulated him.

God's heart was already broken. It has been broken from the foundation of the world. God doesn't get shocked nor does his heart break every time he sees you sin. The God of the universe doesn't have such high hopes for you that it breaks his heart when you don't live up to his expectations. His "expectations" about you were accurate long before you were born. From the foundation of the world, he prepared for Bethlehem. It's done. You've already broken his heart. That's what the cross is all about. On the cross Christ died for you . . . but don't ever forget that you died too.

That brings me to one of the most important memorandums you'll ever receive. You're dead! And just so you know, dead men do bleed.

All my Christian life I've heard messages on mortifying the flesh so that one is "crucified with Christ." They told me that it's hard to die and then suggested certain ways to make it happen—stop smoking, don't let your mind go to places that are tempting, get rid of your idols, stay up and pray all night, sacrifice for Christ, pick up a cross and follow him, be humble, memorize Scripture, pray a lot, and don't think of yourself first. And then there are those who go to the extreme of hair shirts, self-flagellation, or living in a desert cave. Others have mutilated themselves or even, I'm told, actually placed themselves on a real cross with friends driving nails through their hands and feet.

Not only is all of that stuff neurotic, it doesn't work. And it's not even what the Scripture is saying. But even more important, *you're already dead*. As I said in the last chapter, Paul doesn't give a command in Galatians 2; he is stating a fact. You are crucified with Christ.

The man who thought he was (physically) dead was in fact not physically dead yet. He was going to die (the death rate is 100 percent and the statistic is one out of one), but it hadn't happened yet. All the hospital's efforts sought to help him see what was true. He needed to see that he was alive. Paul wants us to see that we're already dead. We have been crucified with Christ.

So what does it mean to be crucified with Christ? How does one live in that reality? What difference will it make? Those are good questions and I'm here to help. The reason I want to help is that being dead has profound implications for our hidden agendas and masks. In fact, if you don't get what I'm going to teach you here, you'll continue to scheme and plan your agendas, and you'll continue to hide behind your masks. At least that's what I do when I forget.

I'm told that playing golf is a matter of attitude. I'm not sure that's true, but I suspect it is. For years I played golf. My friends who played with me during that time say that I never "played golf." I was too bad to call it "playing." The first time I played was on Cape Cod with a pastor friend who said he would teach me. And I was happy to learn. After all, Billy Graham played a lot of golf and, if Mr. Graham did it, it must be spiritual. (Years later I heard Mr. Graham say that he hated golf and only did it because of the ministry involved. I wanted to say, "Thanks a lot! You could have said that years ago and saved me a lot of blood, sweat, and tears.")

That first time I played, my pastor friend started talking about the water hole on the fourth fairway. "I just want to warn you so that when we get there you won't be surprised." When we were playing the first hole, he said, "I know it's not easy, but you haven't seen anything yet. That water hole on the fourth is a corker." On the third hole, he said, "Get ready. The next hole is where even good golfers lose a lot of strokes. It's the water hole."

By the time I got to the fourth hole I was thoroughly intimidated. I lost seven golf balls in that pond and finally just gave up and walked around it, playing on the other side. Do you know what my friend did? He started laughing and said, "I've just taught you the most important lesson you'll ever learn about playing golf. It's not keeping your left arm straight, it's not your stance, and it's not keeping your head down and your eye on the ball. It's what's you think. Do notice that I talked you into losing seven balls. That was to help you remember: It's in your head."

Being crucified with Christ is in your head too. It's an objective fact, but it's also a matter of attitude.

Paul wrote, "I appeal to you therefore, brothers, by the mercies of God, to present your bodies as a living sacrifice, holy and acceptable to God, which is your spiritual worship. Do not be conformed to this world, but be transformed by the *renewal of your mind . . ."* (Romans 12:1–2, emphasis added). The writer of Proverbs said, "For as he thinketh in his heart, so is he" (Proverbs 23:7 KJV).

Now, before we look at some of the implications of being dead as they apply to hidden agendas and masks, it's important to consider how the Holy Spirit leads us to realize that we are dead. Recognizing that death has already happened is hard; just applying spiritual "elbow grease" to the task won't work. But we have a friend in high places. It's the Holy Spirit and Jesus promised (he called the Holy Spirit the "Helper") that he would send him to us to help us. My friend J. D. Greear says that the Holy Spirit is like our pituitary gland. You know it's there, you're glad you've got it, and you don't want to lose it, but you're not exactly sure what it does. Well, the Holy Spirit does a lot. For our purposes here, the Holy Spirit is our teacher, reminder, and enabler.

A number of years ago I suffered from a hip problem. For over a year I walked with a cane. Every time I leaned on one side, I felt an excruciating pain. As long as I was leaning on the other side, sitting, or in bed, there was no problem and no pain. But turn the wrong way and "Ouch!!" That pain was a teacher. I learned to be very careful about the way I walked, how I turned, and the steps I climbed. The pain was also a reminder: "Hey, be careful. Don't lean on that side." But when I did, there was always a kind soul who became my enabler, and would grab my arm and make sure I didn't fall.

The Holy Spirit is like that. Jesus said that the Holy Spirit is the "Spirit of truth" (John 14:17), that "he will teach you all things" (John 14:26), and that he would give us the "gasoline" to do what he reminded and taught us: "But the Helper, the Holy Spirit, whom the Father will send in my name, he will teach you all things and bring to your remembrance all that I have said to you" (John 14:26).

That's a short lesson in the doctrine and reality of the Holy Spirit. The reality behind the doctrine is this: The key to being reasonably free of hidden agendas and masks is remembering you're dead and the key to knowing and applying that is the Holy Spirit.

There are some things we should remember about dead people. Dead people don't have to "do" anything. Dead people don't care what others think about them. Dead people aren't unduly concerned about accumulating stuff. Dead people don't have anything to prove or to fake. They no longer have to be right. And dead people hardly ever have hidden agendas or wear masks. That almost goes without saying. The Scripture says that we are dead and frankly, that's a relief. I'm tired.

Samuel Johnson, the eighteenth-century English writer, heard about a man who was going to be hanged and was said to observe that the prospect of one's own death concentrates one's mind wonderfully. It does. He also said in a letter he wrote to Sir Joshua Reynolds, "That we must all die, we always knew; I wish I had remembered it sooner."[1]

So how does one make the fact of one's death a useful reality in one's life? How do we make the concept practical? One increasingly discerns the reality of one's death by *remembering.*

My friend Paul Zahl wrote a delightful book, *PZ's Panopticon.* Paul, without giving details, wrote that, after thirty-two years of professional religionist service, he had a sudden near-death experience: "It happened at a specific time in a specific place. Everything I think about religion now comes through the Panopticon (a center place of focus where one sees everything else) of that near-death experience. Much of what I had thought about religion prior to my near-death experience changed during it, within a time period of approximately ten minutes. Much of what I had thought about myself changed, too, and again in approximately ten minutes."[2]

Personally, I'm not sure how I feel about out-of-body experiences. They bother me sometimes, but then, I wasn't there. In any case, throughout the book, Dr. Zahl uses the imagery of a dying/dead man who is having an out-of-body experience as he dies. The man looks down from the ceiling and Zahl suggests what the man really needs to hear. In other words, what's really important? What do you say to someone who is almost dead?

The business of the Holy Spirit is to remind you of your own spiritual death in Christ; to apply that memory to your present reality, and then to hammer it home, causing you to live your life with the reminder. Like Paul Zahl's near-death experience, it is the key to living. It is the Panopticon that changes everything you thought about yourself, the world, and your faith. It is what Paul meant when he wrote that we should reckon or consider ourselves dead. The Bible is a practical book on how to live . . . but it is even more practical on how to die or, more accurately, on how to recognize you have already "assumed room temperature."

Let me show you. Considering yourself dead is to discover . . .

What Is Really Important

Do you remember the story Jesus told about the farmer whose farm was incredibly successful (Luke 12)? The farmer was smoking a cigar on the back porch and planning how to deal with his newfound wealth. He was going to tear down his barns and build bigger ones, and then he was going to kick back and enjoy his retirement. He fantasized about the booze, parties, and fun. God said to the man, "Fool! This night your soul is required of you, and the things you have prepared, whose will they be?" (Luke 12:20).

It is said that after the North had taken Richmond during the Civil War, there were literally wagonloads of Confederate money hauled away. Some of the soldiers who had become bored with it all got together a poker game. They played the game with worthless Confederate money, often playing for thousands of dollars a hand. What was important about their poker game? Nothing. Nothing at all.

In our culture we are playing, as it were, a lot of poker games with phony, worthless money. Mark Twain once told a group of wealthy businesspeople that they would one day meet someone who didn't have a dime yet was happy. "Then," he said, "you'll know that you've paid too much for your whistle."

The world lies to us all the time. I actually believed the commercial pushing the hair growth product. They lied. So did those who said that fame, money, and being more religious would make everything okay. I've had a modicum of all three and those folks lied to me too. I thought that if I ate properly, exercised regularly, and stayed away from products bad for my body, I would live a long and healthy life. Instead I found out that I was just like a ship going down with nothing to throw overboard. They lied. And it was the Holy Spirit who reminded me. In that reminder, I was able to "consider myself dead."

All of my life I wanted to be a mega-church pastor. I always served relatively small churches until eventually God told me I didn't have to be a pastor anymore. Not too long ago a member of the pulpit committee of a very large church asked me to consider becoming their pastor. I told him he was crazy, but he said, "Steve, at least pray about it." I did.

"Lord," I prayed, "you know I've always wanted that kind of church. Think of the impact I could make for you and the lives I could touch . . . to say nothing of the money I could make. I would tithe that money and you would get far more than you're getting from me now."

At that moment, God took the blinders off and reminded me of that day in my study when my life came apart. He showed me a picture of angry Christians at a congregational meeting. He showed me the graves beside which I wept and the suicides I had cleaned up. He reminded me of the sleepless night when a drunk called at 3 o'clock in the morning and the times I stayed up worrying about the direction of the church.

I wrote the man on the pulpit committee. "I did as you requested," I wrote in handwriting so shaky I could hardly read it. "I prayed and God said I was crazy to even pray about it. I will, however, be praying for you guys as you seek the right pastor for your church."

The reminder was from the Holy Spirit. When he reminded me about the importance (or lack of it) of serving a mega-church, I repented (i.e., agreed with God) and it was a part of the process of considering myself dead.

Considering yourself dead is also to discover . . .

What Is Going to Last

Paul wrote to the Philippians, "But one thing I do: forgetting what lies behind and straining forward to what lies ahead, I press on toward the goal for the prize of the upward call of God in Christ Jesus . . . and if in anything you think otherwise, God will reveal that also to you"

(Philippians 3:13–15). In other words, a lot of things aren't going to last, but Christ is the same yesterday, today, and forever, and when you die only that will remain. In the great love chapter of the Bible (1 Corinthians 13), Paul wrote that three things would last—faith, hope, and love—and then he pointed out that love was the greatest of the three. Not only that, Paul wrote his friends in Philippi that the Holy Spirit would remind them of what will last and what won't. I have a friend who says that everybody ought to be a part of something that will last longer than they do.

Do you remember when the disciples came to Jesus pointing out the beauty of the buildings and the temple in Jerusalem (Mark 13)? Jesus said that soon they would no longer be there and that "there will not be left one stone upon another that will not be thrown down" (Mark 13:2). Of course, there are other implications to what Jesus said, but one of the important ones is that no matter how big, beautiful, important, or expensive, be careful about attaching yourself to something that won't be here in the future.

We have a young man, Zach Van Dyke, who's a regular participant in Key Life's weekly talk show and video pastor's chats. He is one of the most winsome and authentic Christians I've ever met. I love him and the ways God is using him. When Zach started working with us, he was the youth pastor of a large church here in Orlando. Now, two years later, he is the pastor of a mega-church where thousands of people worship every weekend. That's a pretty heady experience that has never gone to Zach's head. He kids (and we kid him) about being a mega-church pastor.

I don't have time to give you the details, but part of Zach's story is that while he and his girlfriend (now his wife, Kelly) were babysitting, a little boy in the family tragically drowned in the swimming pool. Through that very hard time, the mother of that little boy, Vicki (and a whole lot of others), loved Zach and Kelly. The story is about how the church works when it is really the church.

At any rate, Zach was the "perfect" Christian growing up. His parents are wonderful and they take their faith seriously. Zach grew up in Christian schools and was the model student. That was on the outside. On the inside, it was a different story.

He (and this is true) won the "Christian of the Year" award seven straight years at his Christian school, right up to his graduation from high school. Each year he received a small golden statue inscribed with his name and "Christian of the Year." One of those little statues sits in the middle of the large table in our Key Life studio where we do the weekly talk show. Sometimes (well, a lot of times) we make reference to that statue and kid Zach with, "Of course you're right (or bright or pure) because you're 'Christian of the Year.'"

I recorded the talk show today. Zach was there and I noticed the little statue. It's been there for so long that I hardly even notice it anymore, but today I did. The fake gold is peeling and, frankly, it looks rather shabby and old, on its last legs. Pretty soon, I guess, we'll throw the gold statue in the garbage.

How many "little gold statues" do you have . . . or pictures on your smartphone, degrees on your wall, cash in your bank, homes, and accolades from friends? When you are crucified with Christ, the Holy Spirit reminds you that none of that will last and he hammers it home. Then you repent. When that happens, you begin to realize what it means to die.

Considering yourself dead is also to discover . . .

What Is True

I mentioned the Holy Spirit's job of being a "recaller of truth" (John 14:17, 26). He is that, but his truth is so radical and amazing that we would never believe it or even think of it if the Holy Spirit didn't remind us.

My late friend, Jack Miller (whom I mentioned earlier as founder of World Harvest Mission—now Serge—and originator of the *Sonship* course), used to refer to the fact that we are the "adopted children" of God. That's a wonderful doctrine (Ephesians 1:5; Romans 8:15; Galatians 3:26) and it means, as I wrote earlier, that we are the children of God and live in the "big house." Jack would often say to depressed Christians and sinful ones, "You're acting like an orphan."

Most of us do on occasion. We do that when our ego gets out of control. It happens when we forget that we're forgiven and loved. It happens when we think we'll never get better and God will finally say, "I've had it with you." It happens when we think our sin is too big, our rebellion too strong, and our actions so ugly that even God can't love us anymore. It happens when everybody we care about has turned their backs on us and we're sure that Jesus has too.

One of the hardest things about being a preacher is what happens after you preach. It is a part of the Christian "liturgy" for people to say to the preacher, "Fine sermon, pastor!" and the liturgical response is, "Thank you. I'm glad God could use it." I tell my seminary students that when they get tired of that, they should respond, "Yes, it was a great sermon. In fact, it may the best sermon I've ever preached. Not only that, it may be one of the greatest sermons preached in this church in the last ten years. Let me take this opportunity to congratulate you on your discernment and taste." Generally, that kind of response will break people of the "liturgical" and "phony" habit of saying the same thing over and over again.

I do a lot of speaking and preaching at conferences, seminars, and churches, and, frankly, I'm pretty good at it. And even if I'm not, a lot of people say that I am. On those occasions, when my peacock feathers start flying in the breeze and my ego is out of control, the Holy Spirit whispers, "Child, you're acting like an orphan. Don't you have a daddy? Don't you have a home?" In that supernatural reminder, I learn what it means to be crucified with Christ. It's being slapped upside the head in a way that allows me to see truth. It's the truth that when the sermon (or the life, or the race, or the grade on the exam, or the results of a beauty contest) is bad or good, it doesn't matter. I'm defined by God's love, not by my actions, sins, and reputation. When the Holy Spirit reminds me and I repent, that is dying to self.

Living with What You Just Discovered

Paul wrote something quite amazing: "So you also must consider yourselves dead to sin and alive to God in Christ Jesus. . . . For sin will have no dominion over you, since you are not under law but under grace" (Romans 6:11, 14). That doesn't mean you, in fact, quit sinning. It's just that sin is no longer the defining reality in your life.

If what we say we believe is true (and it is), then every sin I ever committed or thought about committing was covered by the sacrifice of Christ. Not only that, if Paul is right about Christ's righteousness being placed in my account (and he was), then my sin isn't the issue. Should it concern me? Of course it should. Sin is destructive and it hurts people I love and it hurts me. That's why it's sin. Should I obsess about it? Of course not. I'm forgiven and God doesn't keep bringing it up. He keeps loving me and in that love (at least some of the time) I sin less because I'm being molded into the image of Jesus by the chisel of his love.

When Paul wrote that Christ came to save sinners and added "of whom I am the foremost" (1 Timothy 1:15), he was illustrating what it means to be crucified with Christ. It is the reflection of a man who doesn't give a rip about the judgment of others, the accolades of the crowd, or the things everybody who is anybody thinks are important. Knowing that you are crucified with Christ is the reminder over and over again of what matters, what will last, and what is true. Don't let anybody tell you to be more religious and thereby be crucified with Christ. They don't know what they're talking about. You are *already* crucified with Christ. You don't have to have a hidden agenda and you don't have to wear a mask. You're loved and acceptable before the God of the universe . . . and that makes you dangerous.

A number of years ago I wrote a "Trinitarian Trilogy": *If God Is in Charge* (theology), *If Jesus Has Come* (Christology), and *Follow the Wind* (pneumatology). (The title of that third book was initially supposed to be *If the Spirit Is Here*.) At any rate, all three books were designed to answer the question, "So what?" If God, Christ, and the Holy Spirit, then . . .

When I wrote the first book, I suggested to the editor that if he would let me title it what I wanted, we wouldn't have to do the book. I told him we would just send out the title and it would be enough. He looked at me puzzled and said, "Well, what would you call it?" I said, "Let's title it, *If God Is in Charge . . . What the Hell!*" He didn't think that was very funny. However, it was the essence of the book.

What follows has never been written in a Christian book before, so pay attention.

Years later I slipped and used the above-mentioned phrase. One of my staff members, George Abihider, said, "Steve, you have to be careful. We're going to have a major donor here sometime and they'll be shocked. Stay there," he said, "and I'll be right back." A few minutes later, George was grinning when he handed me a piece of paper with a Latin phrase on it: *Quid Inferorum*. George said, "Now you can say it in Latin. Nobody will know you're cussing and they'll even think you're smart."

So let me leave you with the phrase, *Quid Inferorum*.

Being crucified with Christ doesn't mean—contrary to the Desert Fathers (whom I read and like a lot)—to never be involved in what's not important, to never engage in what won't last, and to refuse to have anything to do with anybody who doesn't believe what is true. Even if you're dead, you can't be an outsider of the human race. But it does mean that you will gradually be able to put a proper price tag on all that. As the Holy Spirit does that—reminds you that you don't have to give a rip about what everybody thinks—it will bring to mind the sovereignty of God, the love of Christ, and the message of the Holy Spirit. As you agree, bit by bit, you'll die (or recognize that you already have), bit by bit.

It's saying with all your heart: *Quid Inferorum*.

I just taught you how to cuss.

Don't thank me. I was glad to help.

Behind the Mask

1. What does being "crucified with Christ" mean to you?

2. "Dead people don't have to 'do' anything. Dead people don't care what others think about them. Dead people don't have anything to prove or to fake. Dead people hardly ever have hidden agendas or wear masks." How is this a relief?

3. How is knowing you are crucified with Christ a reminder of what matters, what will last, and what is true?

4. How does being loved and acceptable before God make you dangerous?

Background Scriptures: Romans 6:10–14; Philippians 3:13–15; 1 Corinthians 13

Note to small group leaders: Refer to these Scriptures as needed during your discussion, along with Scripture passages in the chapter.

CHAPTER 7

Gotcha!

"Judge not, that you be not judged. For with the judgment you pronounce you will be judged, and with the measure you use, it will be measured to you." (Matthew 7:1–2)

You would have liked my father. Everybody liked my father. I'm not sure why they did. He never finished high school and didn't have any degrees. He was a drunk and would disappear from the company where he worked sometimes for a week at a time. He was a gambler and womanizer. My father was also a bastard (no, not the profane one but the real one) in the days when that simply wasn't acceptable. He was raised by a single mother. My father had very little with which to commend himself.

Though he was someone with very little formal education, my father rose to an executive position with his company. Even when he would disappear, "the powers that be" would overlook those periods and pretend they hadn't happened. My father was a gambler but quite good at it. When pool hustlers would come through town, he would be called and a crowd would gather to watch with great enthusiasm as my father "cleaned the clock" of the pool hustler. A friend of mine said that whenever someone asked, "Who's the best pool player in town?" without hesitation, the answer would always be, "Brownie . . . when he's sober." Then there was always the follow-up question, "Well, who's the second best pool player?" The answer was always, "Brownie . . . when he's drunk." The women with whom he had affairs loved him, even knowing that he had betrayed them.

My father loved my brother and me without reservation. If we weren't there, he thought it was impossible to have a party. He showed off our pictures and bragged on us to anybody who would listen. He only spanked me twice that I can remember and both times he cried while doing it. When I almost blew up an elderly lady one night—I honestly didn't see her in that rocking chair when I threw the cherry bomb on her porch —my father wasn't happy, but he still loved me, going with me to the home to apologize and standing with me when I went to the police. When he died, a very long line of people came to offer their condolences, and the comment made more often than any other to my brother and me was, "Do you boys know how much your daddy loved you?" We did.

There's one other thing you should know about my father. He hardly ever went to church, talked about God, or had anything to do with Christianity. When my brother or I would "perform" at a church function, he would sit in the back and leave when we finished. But that was pretty much it.

Do you know why he had so little to do with the church? It had nothing to do with "those hypocrites" or a lack of belief. It was because my father didn't think he was good enough. He missed the main message of the Christian faith and almost missed Jesus. I'm so thankful for the physician who said to my father, "Mr. Brown, you have about three months to live. We're going to pray and then I'm going to tell you something more important than what I just told you." That man told my father about Jesus—the Jesus who came for the sick and sinful, not the good. My father heard, was surprised, and then "ran to Jesus."

I'll introduce you to my father when we all get Home.

I've often wondered why my father was so beloved by so many people. It wasn't because he was good at his job. (He was, though. When he retired, the company had to hire three people to replace him.) It wasn't because he was such a skillful pool and card player. (He was, though. After all these years, the old folks in my hometown still tell stories about his skill.) It wasn't because he had friends in low (and high) places and was loyal to them. (He did and he was, though. I don't think I've ever seen so many drunks and executives cry at a funeral.)

So why did everybody love him? They loved him for the same reason he didn't go to church. They loved him because he didn't think he was good enough. When I was growing up, I never heard my father say negative things about the church or church members. In fact, I don't think I ever heard him say anything critical about anybody. (Well, he was a Democrat and wasn't altogether pleased with Truman. He would say, "Once I was a Democrat as happy as could be . . . Now I'm a Republican and wish Truman was a tree." Then he would laugh. He never, by the way, became a

Republican.) The reason my father was never critical or condemning of people was because he always thought others were a lot better than he was. And the reason he never went to church wasn't that the church was at fault; he felt he was. The church was for good people, and my father knew he wasn't good.

The reason I'm telling you this is that my father, even though most of the time he wasn't a Christian, modeled (at least in relationships) what I want to talk about in this chapter. He treated others as better than he was. Jesus said in Luke 14 that we should do the same thing. He said that, when invited to a wedding banquet, we should take the lowest place. That's where my father always sat. He believed that was where he belonged. Paul said, "In humility count others more significant than yourselves" (Philippians 2:3). My father modeled that and it affected how he treated people.

Do you know why we wear masks and have hidden agendas? It's because revealing the reality behind the mask might destroy the self-image we're trying to maintain—that we're really good people, obedient Christians, and compassionate souls who love kittens and people. Anything other than that is too threatening to consider. If we've looked behind the masks and considered the destruction that would be caused by our hidden agendas if people knew the truth, it's way too threatening. People would know we aren't really good people, obedient Christians, and compassionate souls who love kittens and people.

So, tragically, the church becomes a place where strangers gather and pretend a love we don't have and fake a compassion we don't feel. One simply can't love someone they don't know or feel compassion for one whose pain is hidden. In other words, you can't love and feel compassion for a mask.

Gotcha!

Edward Wallis Hoch's poem was first published in *The Marion Record* (Kansas) in the early twentieth century, and you've probably heard it quoted a thousand times. It is true . . . sort of:

> There is so much good in the worst of us,
> And so much bad in the best of us,
> That it hardly behooves any of us
> To talk about the rest of us.

There is a sense in which my father had to be a drunk before he could be a Christian. He had to fail in order to know what it's like to be really loved. He had to face the humiliation of his mask being ripped off (everybody knew about him) to have a heart that could care for others. In other words, he had to be bad to be good.

You do too.

I've often joked about praying for Christians who are self-righteous, critical, and dismissive of others who don't "live up" to their standards (masks). I've joked about praying that they'd somehow get drunk in a public place and make a fool out of themselves, confessing their deepest and darkest secrets to people they're trying to impress or judge. But I'm not totally joking. Sometimes I think that the fastest way to see genuine renewal and revival in the church would be for us to throw a church-wide party with the express purpose of everybody getting plastered. The masks would have to come off, and I suspect the Pharisees in the church would be better for it. I know this one would.

Now before we get to some specifics, I feel constrained to say something to unbelievers who are reading this book. (I don't have the faintest idea why you would want to read this book, but some always do.) You're at least as bad as we Christians are and, in some cases, worse. So don't go self-righteous on those "judgmental, arrogant, and condemning Christians." You do it too! You just use a different standard to beat up others—it's called political correctness and it can destroy a nation. The arrogance and self-righteousness expressed by political leaders, pundits, and political and social commentators are nothing less than astounding. Not only that, social media has taken what once was one person expressing shock and disappointment about another to a viral level, until we're now living in the most self-righteous, arrogant, and shallow nation in the history of the world. Nobody cuts anybody any slack lest people will think we are "like them." The hidden agendas we plan and the masks we wear are designed to never let something like that happen.

But then, I guess I don't have standing to tell unbelievers what to do. But if you're a Christian, you're my family and we should be better than that. I wish more of us were like my drunk father. I wish I were. Not because of the drinking, but because the drinking meant my father couldn't wear a mask.

My father was a drunk, and because he and everybody else knew he was he didn't have anything to protect, he didn't have to pretend to play a role, he didn't have to hide, and he was the most forgiving and unconditionally accepting man I've ever known.

Nothing to Protect

Have you ever thought about how much time and effort we spend protecting things? It's why we have banks, store up gold, have insurance, carry guns, buy alarm systems and, maybe more important, why we wear masks. I have some friends who lived in a rather unsafe area and were robbed three times. Well, actually, only two times. The first robber broke into their house and took most of their valuables. The second robber got the rest. When the third robber broke in and went to the silver cabinet, there wasn't any silver. Instead there was a note that read, "Sorry, the others got it all. God loves you anyway." With the note, they left a small booklet describing the love of Jesus for sinners. They were delighted when they got home from church to find that they had been robbed again and that the thief had taken the note and the booklet.

There is a freedom in not having anything to protect. The Bible says that Jesus "made himself nothing" (Philippians 2:7 NIV). He protected nothing. Paul told his detractors in 1 Corinthians 4:3 that it didn't matter to him what they said about him. Why was that? Because he didn't have anything to protect. For our purposes here, it is important that Christians remember that they don't have to protect their good name, image, or Christian witness.

There is an old story about a man taking a cross-country train in India. That particular train was known to have thieves who often stole from passengers. This man had everything he owned in a suitcase and he put it in the rack above his seat. He was determined to stay awake to protect his "stuff." At three in the morning, the man's eyes grew heavy and he drifted off for just a moment. When he opened his eyes, his suitcase was gone. "Thank God," he said. "Now I can get some sleep."

In the last chapter I talked about being crucified with Christ. Dead people, in fact, don't have to protect anything anymore. My father's drinking meant that he didn't have to wear a mask to protect his image and reputation. His drinking meant he had to die to all that. The result was that he had a kind of quiet peace about him. It was because he didn't have anything to protect.

No Pretending to Play a Role

We might not be drunks (someone said that we should not be too critical of those whose sin is different from our sin) but, as I understand it, when we publicly declared our relationship to Christ in baptism or church membership, we properly said to the world, "I'm needy, sinful, and desperate." We still are. It is no accident that Paul, when he proclaimed he was a sinner, didn't say he "used to be a really bad sinner" or that he was working on it and getting better. He said (to paraphrase), "I *am* the chief, the worst, the most sinful of the whole bunch" (1 Timothy 1:15). My father could say that too and, when he did, he was free of his mask . . . maybe more so than the church members he thought were better than they were.

I didn't vote for Bill Clinton and probably wouldn't vote for his wife either. I'm a Republican and would vote for the Devil if his party affiliation were the same as mine. (Well, maybe not. But close.) But there is something I find winsome about former President Clinton, and it's the reason he's consistently in the top three on those lists of the most popular people in the world.

When he went through the impeachment trial and came out on the other side, he held a press conference. One of the reporters asked if he planned to forgive those who had instituted his trial. Clinton thought for a moment and said, "Yes, people who need forgiveness must forgive." As embarrassing as the things he had done were, it put him in a place of no longer having to pretend to be a "good Baptist." At least there, he didn't have to wear a mask.

No Hiding

If you're a smoker and a preacher, let me give you some advice. Never announce publicly in a worship service that you've stopped smoking. The first and last time I did that, the congregation applauded. Then people started sending me chewing gum and candy, and telling me that they were praying for me. I did really well with the candy, chewing gum, and prayers . . . for three days. That's when I started sneaking. Three or four times a day I would leave my office—telling my secretary a lie about where I was going—and drive up into the hills above Boston to smoke two or three cigarettes.

But that's not the worst part. I would then go into the pulpit on Sundays to preach sermons on honesty and authenticity. I felt like a salesman for a hair restoration medication wearing a toupee. I suspect there were other times when I didn't "walk the talk" and model the things I taught (I still struggle with that), but this was over the top. After a while I just couldn't do it anymore. I remember going into the pulpit one Sunday morning and saying to the congregation, "Listen up. I have an important announcement to make." Everybody got quiet as I continued, "I've started smoking again. Now let us pray."

The congregation wasn't that happy . . . but I was. I wasn't only happy. I was free. In that freedom, I saved a fortune not having to buy breath mints and cologne to hide my smoking, to say nothing of the money I saved in gasoline driving up into the hills above Boston to smoke. But far more important than that, I didn't have to hide my sin. Everybody knew.

In Romans 7 Paul makes his confession, "For I do not do the good I want, but the evil I do not want is what I keep on doing" (Romans 7:19). At first I thought, *Paul, I don't believe I would have said that. That's crazy!* Then I realized it was crazy . . . crazy like a fox. Aside from Paul clearly showing his weakness and need for Christ, if anyone saw Paul being selfish, in his pride bragging about what he had done for Christ (as in 2 Corinthians 11), or refusing to speak to or work with his brother, Barnabas, nobody would be surprised. Paul was free to be what he was even if it wasn't pretty.

Not too long ago on our weekly talk show, we interviewed Jennifer Knapp about her book, *Facing the Music: My Story.*[1] Frankly, I had no idea who Jennifer Knapp was but I think I was the only person in the universe who didn't. My staff explained that she had been a very successful Christian musician. She had then left the Christian music scene and disappeared for a number of years only to emerge with the announcement that she was a lesbian. Christians were angry and very few, if any, churches lined up to have her sing. Jennifer's book is the record of her childhood, her love for music, and the trials of singing to people who, if they knew the truth, would never have come to her concerts. In the book she makes it clear that she hasn't given up hope or her faith.

When my staff told me whom I would be interviewing and explained who she was, I wasn't very comfortable with it. I hold orthodox, traditional, and, I might say, biblical views on human sexuality, and I wasn't sure I could pull off an interview with Jennifer Knapp that wouldn't sound like just more of the hatred, rejection, and vitriol she had experienced from many Christians. I didn't want to compromise the truth I knew and, at the same time, I didn't want to make the talk show into an hour of throwing rocks, debating her on the evil of her position, and telling her that she needed to repent. As a friend of mine says, "You see a lot of fat preachers yelling at gay folks but you see very few gay folks yelling at fat preachers." I didn't want to fit that mold. So instead, I looked to Jesus as my model. And you know what? It was a delightful hour. I didn't define Jennifer by her sexuality (any more than I would define anybody else by their sin or by what they do) and she didn't define me by the anger and hatred she had experienced in the past. We were two professing Christians—both of us sinful, needy, and loved by Jesus—caring about each other. After the interview, Jennifer said that she loved the time. Of course she did! She didn't have to hide. There is something refreshing about taking off your mask and being who you are . . . the good and the bad, the sin and the faithfulness, and the failure and the success.

Forgiving and Unconditionally Accepting

Simply because my father didn't have to protect, pretend, or hide, in very real sense he found radical obedience in at least one area: Jesus's command to forgive.

I don't know about you, but forgiveness is hard for me. Well, it isn't hard when the wrong done to me is a tiny thing. If you get angry with me, don't speak to me, or make jokes about me, I appear to be Saint Stephen in my quickness to forgive. And if you properly repent on your knees before me for what you've done, there is hardly anything I won't forgive. But if you disrespect, devalue, dishonor, or dismiss me, and then don't even care that you have, I become a serial killer. The problem is that Jesus gives me no wiggle room even then.

You will remember Matthew 18:21–35, when Peter asked Jesus how often he should forgive some twit who had done bad things to him. "I've already forgiven him seven times," Peter told Jesus, "and that seems reasonable." Jesus's response was unexpected. He told Peter that he should forgive him "seventy times seven" (i.e., unlimited) times. Then Jesus told Peter a story that is so radical and scary that, from then on, Peter would never have been able to withhold forgiveness without feeling guilty about it. In the prayer Jesus taught his disciples to pray, he said that we should ask for forgiveness as we forgive others (Matthew 6:12). Just to make sure that we got it, he expanded on forgiveness right after teaching the prayer (Matthew 6:14–15).

I learned to forgive from my father. Do you know why? Because, again, he didn't think he was as good as everybody else. People who feel that way forgive others who also aren't good enough. You have to know you're bad to be good (i.e., forgiving). That connects to the truth in the prayer Jesus taught that we should forgive *as* we've been forgiven.

I have a friend who allowed a "root of bitterness" to spring up in his life and he can't forgive those who have hurt him deeply. I'll spare you the details, but what was done to him was horrible. My friend wanted me to join him in judgment and condemnation. I didn't, and he noticed: "What do you want me to do, forgive? Are you crazy? How do you expect me to do that?"

"The only way I know for you to do that," I told him, "is go out and sin against God as greatly as those people have sinned against you. Then when God forgives you—and he will—you'll be able to forgive them. I don't know any other way because only those who have been forgiven can forgive, and they can only forgive to the degree to which they have been forgiven."

Of course, my friend doesn't have to go out and sin. He's already doing that. And he has sinned against God far more than those people have sinned against my friend.

I have a "hit list" on my prayer list of people I pray get the fever and die or, at least, get the hives. I tell God that I know what he wants from me but I just can't do what he wants. Then I pray that he bless the ones for whom I just prayed a curse. And then, reluctantly, I ask that he bless them regardless of my feelings and conform my heart to the request. As I write this, there are only two people on my "hit list" and by the time you read this, they won't be there. You see, I'm learning to forgive as I remember my father and then think of the cross on which I hung the Son of God. I can forgive. Nothing removes the masks on people more than the need to forgive, and I can't forgive until I take mine off.

I suspect that as you've read this, you've been somewhat troubled by what I've written. I did say that a good way to have an awakening in the church was to have a party where everybody got plastered. I did use my father's pre-Christian sin and drunkenness to advocate how Christians should live. I did say that Christians ought to emulate my father. And I did say that Christians should be open about their sin.

That is all true; but listen, I didn't say what you think I said.

A number of years ago I spoke in South America for the annual conference of a very large mission organization. During the week I taught the doctrines of grace and I was also very honest (in appropriate ways) about my own sin, failure, and desperation. At the final session (just before we celebrated Holy Communion together) there was a time when the missionaries could stand up and give their "witness" about what God had done in their lives during the week. In some ways, it was an incredible week. We had all "heard the sound of sandaled feet" in our midst, and many who stood up talked about what had happened to them, often with tears.

About a half hour into that session, a man stood up. I could tell by the angry look on his face that he was not very happy. "You are not going to like what I'm going to say," he said, looking around the conference hall, "but somebody has to say it. I have been quite disturbed this week. The speaker has dismissed the holiness of God, minimized the horror of sin, bragged about his own sin, and brought shame on the name of Christ."

It got very quiet. (I immediately commenced to pray that the man get the hives. Of course not!) I thought about what he said and started thinking about what I had been teaching and why he had so misunderstood. I wanted to go back and correct what I taught and even repent of some of it. That was when another missionary stood up. "I know what my brother is saying, but I think he missed the point. The reason for all the tears and the changed lives isn't because Steve lowered the standards. Just the opposite. I would remind my brother that it is one thing to lower the standards and it is quite another to confess that one doesn't live up to them. Steve didn't lower the standards; he just suggested that it was, as with Paul, a struggle to live up to them. As I understand it, that is the first step to renewal."

It is.

The psalmist said that the law of God was perfect. God's commandments are clear and the best way to live. Sin isn't sin because it's nasty, improper, or just not done. Sin is sin because it's destructive, dark, and frightening. That goes without saying. It also goes without saying that Jesus gives us the power to be different and to live better . . . sometimes. The point I'm making is that our masks and hidden agendas—religious, political, and social—lead to a self-righteousness that robs the church (and even the country) of everything that is important and good. We are so busy playing "Gotcha!" that we don't have time to be honest, to listen, and to hold up one another's arms. That's probably not going to change in the country or the world, but God's people are better than that. In fact, that truth has important implications for the purpose of God's people in the world. We'll talk about that in a later chapter but, for now, remember that when Christians play "Gotcha!" we violate the very essence of our faith.

I can't believe that this old Republican is going to bring up Bill Clinton again. My friend Tony Campolo, who is a friend of the former president, told me once that President Clinton articulated the gospel of Jesus Christ about as well as anybody he knew. That surprised me until I read Luke 7, where the prostitute was welcomed by Jesus, forgiven, and affirmed. Sometimes it is easier for great sinners to get to Jesus than "great" Christians. Almost everybody knows the former president's sins and Clinton has probably given up trying to redeem his reputation. That mask is off.

I suppose Christians should be thankful for Bill Clinton. His sin gave Christians (and many others) the best opportunity in years to feel self-righteous. "I'm bad, but he's worse." "How *could* he?" "Character matters." "We need leaders who model righteousness." Before, Christians were accused of being judgmental, condemning, and greedy. But this time, we were on the right side of the issue and everybody knew it.

There's some truth to that except for one thing. In our self-righteousness, we missed maybe the greatest opportunity in this century for Christians to make a powerful witness for Christ. What do you think would have happened if, after Clinton's relationship with Monica became public,

Christians said, "Yeah, that's bad and I'm sorry, but it could have been me. In fact, I'm capable of so much worse than that. And you know what? Jesus still likes me. Want to know why?"

Of course, we didn't do that. Self-righteousness won that one.

The late Swiss psychiatrist, Paul Tournier, was once asked if he knew Christians who were hypocrites and didn't live up to their faith. He didn't give any details—sometimes details are inappropriate and not required except to those very few we've learned to trust—but he was clear. "Of course," he replied. "Me."

Behind the Mask

1. What would happen if you revealed the reality behind your masks? What would that do to your self-image?
2. Is it true in your experience that the "church is a place where strangers gather and pretend a love we don't have and fake a compassion we don't feel"?
3. How does hiding our pain hurt us and those we love?
4. How would you live your life differently if you didn't have to protect, pretend, and hide? What would it free you up to do instead?
5. How do we forgive others who also aren't good enough?
6. How does self-righteousness (the result of our masks and hidden agendas) rob the church? What does it rob the church of?

Background Scriptures: Matthew 7:1–2; Luke 14; Philippians 2:3–8; Romans 7; Matthew 18:21–35; Matthew 6:12–15

Note to small group leaders: Refer to these Scriptures as needed during your discussion, along with Scripture passages in the chapter.

CHAPTER 8

When Doctrine Sings the "Hallelujah Chorus"

. . . the household of God, which is the church of the living God, a pillar and buttress of the truth. (1 Timothy 3:15)

In the opening passage of his biography of Jesus, Luke wrote, "Inasmuch as many have undertaken to compile a narrative of the things that have been accomplished among us, just as those who from the beginning were eyewitnesses and ministers of the word have delivered them to us, it seemed good to me also, having followed all things closely for some time past, to write an orderly account for you, most excellent Theophilus, that you may have certainty concerning the things you have been taught" (Luke 1:1–4).

That's what I plan to do in this chapter. I want to provide a narrative of what has been accomplished among us. It will be in the form of truth propositions incredibly relevant to the hidden agendas we promote and the masks we wear.

In a piece in *Christianity Today*, Chuck Colson and Timothy George wrote about Francis Schaeffer and his impact in warning the church against succumbing to the relativism that had conquered the world. "Historic Christianity, biblical Christianity," they wrote, quoting Dr. Schaeffer, "believes that Christianity is not just doctrinal truth, but flaming truth—true to what is there, true to the great final environment, the infinite-personal God."[1] Dr. Schaeffer called that truth "true truth."

When I was in seminary at Boston University, the late Clarence Jordan (founder of Koinonia Farm in Georgia and author of the *Cotton Patch* paraphrase of the Bible) was one of the chapel speakers. Because of his high view of Scripture (he was a Greek scholar) and because he believed every word of the Bible, I was surprised that they invited him. Boston University was big on social ethics but not so much on Scripture (it was liberal "just this side of wacko"). I suspect they decided to give Jordan a pass on the Scripture thing because of his effective work with the poor at Koinonia Farm. At any rate, I'll never forget what Clarence Jordan said in that chapel. He said that, because of his doctorate in Greek and his high view of Scripture, he was invited to speak at a lot of conservative churches in the Americus area in Georgia "until they found out that I 'really' believed every word of Scripture and intended to take it seriously and live it out. Then," he said in his colorful way, "I was about as welcome as a wet shaggy dog shaking himself at the Miss America Pageant."

There is often a disconnect between what we say we believe and what we really believe. That's true of everybody, but it can especially be true of Christians. For instance, because of my fairly radical view of grace (we'll talk about it in a minute) I'm often told, "Steve, that's dangerous. Where do you draw the line?" In other words, those people who always want to draw the line don't really believe in grace. Once the line is drawn, you don't have grace. It looks like this: I believe that God is my Father—but I'm still scared. I believe that God is kind and gentle—but I still tremble in his presence. I believe that God is in charge and good all the time—but I still "kick against the goads" of the circumstances of my life. I believe that I'm forgiven—but I still feel guilty. I believe that God likes me better than he likes you—but I still feel on the outside.

At a church I once served, each Sunday a local drug rehabilitation ministry brought a busload of residential clients to our worship service. If you had seen them marching into our proper Presbyterian church, you would have been quite surprised. But they kept coming and many of those guys became Christians. The problem was that some of them looked like Hell's Angels on steroids. My wife and I have two wonderful daughters who were teenagers at the time and one of the elders (one of my closest friends) did too. One Sunday morning my elder friend came into my office, obviously agitated. "Steve," he said, "some of those guys in the drug ministry are flirting with my daughters and it scares me." They had been doing that with my daughters too. Neither of us was altogether happy with Hell's Angel types even looking at our daughters.

"I'm with you," I said to my friend. "It bothers me too. Frankly, I'm more worried about it than you are. But, Charlie, what about Jesus?"

He replied, "Oh, spit!" and walked out of my office. Not only that, he and I both (because of Jesus) became far more welcoming to the guys who were being bussed from that ministry to our church. We even grew to love them.

What follows is "true truth." It isn't true because it works, because I feel good (or bad) about it, or because I like it (or don't). It's "What about Jesus?" truth that is true because it's true. It works, affects my life, and sometimes causes me to break out in song *because* it's true, not the other way around. Truth is true not because it works, but it works because it's true. Whether or not I believe, live, and apply true truth is irrelevant.

Justification

The first truth has to do with a legal matter. Theologians call it "justification" but you can call it . . . getting off scot-free without a fine, a record, or any legal consequences whatsoever—even when you're guilty as sin.

Do you remember the story I told you in chapter 4 about my lawyer friend who backed into a van? (You don't? You really need to take notes. You will be tested on this material.) My friend told me that he would never have to pay a fine, go to traffic school, or be found guilty. He asked for a trial but the van owner's van wasn't damaged that badly and neither the van owner nor the police officer would have time to come to a trial. So he said the whole thing would be dismissed.

Subsequent to that incident, I talked with my friend and kiddingly put some doubts in his mind about both the ethics and wisdom of his actions. "You have the money. Why don't you just admit that you did it and pay the fine? That would be the 'Christian thing to do.' Further," I said, "if the van owner or the police officer shows, they'll tell the court that you backed into the van and you won't have a prayer. That will cause the judge to wonder why you asked for a trial in the first place and when he realizes your scheme, he'll probably throw you in jail."

Over time my lawyer friend became a bit worried. This morning I got an email from him: "Hey, Brown," he said, "nobody showed, my case was dismissed without my saying a word, I don't have to pay a fine or go to traffic school. So there!"

The accusers didn't show. Paul wrote in Romans that we won't ever be condemned either, and for the same reason: "Then what becomes of our boasting? It is excluded. By what kind of law? By a law of works? No, but by the law of faith. For we hold that one is justified by faith apart from works of the law" (Romans 3:27–28). "Therefore, since we have been justified by faith, we have peace with God through our Lord Jesus Christ" (Romans 5:1). "There is therefore now no condemnation for those who are in Christ Jesus. For the law of the Spirit of life has set you free in Christ Jesus from the law of sin and death" (Romans 8:1–2).

We will go to trial but, because of Christ's sacrifice, there won't be any accusers. The blood of Christ was sufficient to pay the penalty for every lie you ever told or will tell, every sin you ever committed or will commit, every person you ever hurt or will hurt, every lustful thought or action you've had or will have, every greedy or angry thought you've had or will have, and every betrayal you ever perpetrated or will perpetrate. It's not just your past that has been legally covered; it's your present and your future. When Jesus said on the cross, "It is finished!" it was finished . . . all of it.

When Christians sing the hymn, "Jesus Paid It All," we sing with great gusto because he really did pay it all. We are in fact declared innocent and Jesus was declared guilty. It doesn't matter how we feel about it or how much guilt we carry. It's a legal fact and it's settled. You have been judged and found innocent. Deal with it.

Imputation

The second propositional truth is that we are clothed. Theologians call it "imputation" but you can call it . . . my new pair of shoes.

I talked about imputation in a previous chapter but let me flesh it out a bit here.

When Martin Luther was asked if we bring nothing to the table, he said that of course we bring something . . . we bring our sin. That's true. But when we went to that table, we traded in our sin for something far better—the goodness, righteousness, obedience, and purity of the One who took our sin to the cross.

Before you go to bed tonight, get your Bible and read Romans 5:12–21. If that doesn't cause you to sing the "Hallelujah Chorus," there's something wrong with you. The Bible teaches that we can go boldly into the throne room of a sovereign and scary God (Hebrews 4:16), that you can dance and sing before that God (even if you're a Presbyterian and can't dance, or an Anglican and can't sing), and that you need never be ashamed before him (or anybody else) again, ever. Why is that? Because you've worked hard to please that God? Because you've become so much better that you're willing to risk it? Because you're so smart and beautiful? Are you crazy? It's because you are covered from head to toe in the righteousness of Christ. Every time God looks at you, he sees Jesus.

The word *imputed* means "accredited." If you had money and put it in my account, you imputed that money to me. The Bible says that what is imputed to your account is the earned perfection of Jesus. It doesn't matter what you earned or didn't earn on your own; his perfection is yours and that changes everything.

A very rich man told me once that he believed in what I taught and that he was going to stand behind me. "Wherever you go, whatever you do, and whatever you dream, I'll pay for it and cover your back." I felt as if I had rubbed an ancient lamp and a genie had emerged to give me the world on a platter. It only lasted for two days before I had offended him with something I said. He withdrew the offer.

Jesus never withdrew the offer. As the father in the prodigal son story (Luke 15) said to the son who'd stayed home, "Everything I have is yours." Everything that Jesus had in terms of perfection, goodness, and purity has been given to us. I don't care how much you think I'm "ugly and my mother dresses me funny." The only one who counts has not only covered me, he has clothed me. *Simul justus et peccator* (I thought I would throw in a bit of Latin there so you would think I'm smart . . . yet another mask for which I must repent) is Martin Luther's phrase and it means "righteous and at the same time a sinner." That's true. I'm both a saint and a sinner. I'm a sinner because, well, I sin. I'm a saint because my sin is covered by the finished work of Christ and because he has given me his righteousness. Both are gifts and I didn't do anything to get either one of them.

It doesn't matter how you feel about what I just told you. The deal is done. You've traded in your dirty rags (sin) for a magnificent and costly "robe of righteousness." Every time you pray, everything you do, everything you are, God sees you as righteous.

Adoption

That brings me to another truth, the doctrine of belonging. Theologians call it "adoption" but you can call it . . . I have a daddy and a home.

We talked about this doctrine in chapter 6 (again, you will be tested on this material) when we saw that we were adopted out of one kingdom (a kingdom of darkness with an abusive father) into another kingdom (a kingdom of light with a benevolent and kind father). Galatians 4:3–7 says, "In the same way we also, when we were children, were enslaved to the elementary principles of the world. But when the fullness of time had come, God sent forth his Son, born of woman, born under the law, to redeem those who were under the law, so that we might receive adoption as sons. And because you are sons, God has sent the Spirit of his Son into our hearts, crying, 'Abba! Father!' So you are no longer a slave, but a son, and if a son, then an heir through God."

I have a friend who adopted a teenager and made her a part of the family. (I know, I know, he was a bit crazy!) I was invited to his home for dinner shortly after the adoption. After spending an evening with my friend and his family, I saw why he had adopted this girl. She was perfect, almost like a "Stepford" daughter. She was quick to help her adoptive mother prepare the meal; she washed the dishes; she said, "Yes, ma'am" or "No, ma'am" or "Yes, sir," or "No, sir" whenever she addressed someone older. Their adopted daughter smiled much of the time, never said anything angry, and didn't act sullen. I thought that my friend had gone to a meat locker (as Dave Barry said about Disney) where they kept frozen teenagers from the fifties, thawed her out, and took her home. She was a delight but she also was, for a teenager, quite weird.

I felt better when I was invited back to my friend's house for dinner some six months later. His daughter was "normal." (Note: A "normal" teenager is different from a "normal" person.) In other words, she was slow to obey, quick to get angry, and quite rebellious. On occasion she was sullen and hard to hug. (It's hard to hug a stiff kid.) I saw a girl who was a curious mix of laughter and tears, rebellion and obedience, and ups and downs.

What was the difference between my first visit to that home and the second? The first time I was there, the adopted daughter was doing her best to please the father because she believed that he would kick her out if she didn't and she would be an orphan again. By the time I got there the second time, she had discovered a great truth: her father would never kick her out . . . ever. It made her worse, but it also made her better.

Sanctification

That brings up the final doctrine. Theologians call it "sanctification" but you can call it . . . getting better.

Just so you know, the biblical view of "getting better" isn't what you think it is. Getting better is never about stopping smoking, drinking, or lying, or hanging out with those who do. Getting better means getting loved. And it has important implications for our discussion of masks and hidden agendas.

The word "sanctification" is from the Middle English and Latin words for "being set apart." Biblically it means "being set apart for a holy purpose." In other words, as Paul put it, "And because of him you are in Christ Jesus, who became to us wisdom from God, righteousness and sanctification and redemption, so that, as it is written, 'Let the one who boasts, boast in the Lord'" (1 Corinthians 1:30–31). Christians to whom the letters of the New Testament are addressed are often called "saints." That doesn't mean they are better than other Christians or more successful in their walk with Christ than an ordinary, average, run-of-the-mill believer. It simply means they are set apart for God and his purposes.

While sanctification does point to a process of getting better that works out in all Christians' lives, it always starts with the fact of who we are. All Christians are saints . . . from the new Christian who is still smoking pot to the mature Christian who has nothing to do with smoke unless it's incense, from the mean-streaked Christian who doesn't "play well with others" to the Christian who is warm and fuzzy to everybody, from the Christian who struggles to the Christian who has given up because she can't do it anymore, to the Christian whose only known sin is that he didn't floss that morning. In other words, at least in its basic meaning, all Christians are saints.

There is an old sermon illustration about a king who had a very unruly son. The boy was so bad that he ran through a long list of tutors, all of whom quit in frustration, telling the king that the boy was simply too rebellious to teach or train. There was one final tutor in the kingdom not yet tried. The king called this man and gave him the job of tutoring his son. Within a week the boy turned respectful and teachable. The king asked the tutor what in the world he had done. "It's simple," the tutor said. "I got a piece of cloth in royal purple and pinned it to his shirt. Then I said to him, 'Son, remember who you are. Every time you look at the royal purple, remember who you are.'"

Now let me say a word about sanctification as a process through which the Christian gets better and better. Sanctification is what leads us into obedience, goodness, and faithfulness, according to the New Testament. Sanctification is a one-time thing that happens when we receive our justification, but it is also a process. The writer of Hebrews put it this way: "For by a single offering he has perfected for all time those who are being sanctified" (Hebrews 10:14). In other words, there is the legal fact of sanctification ("perfected for all time") and then there is the process of being sanctified ("those *who are being* sanctified").

If you read that part and you're thinking you must try harder, work longer, pray more, serve better, and study deeper, you'll "hit a wall"—one I hit quite often. All of that is what hidden agendas are about and what masks are made of. Why is that? Because we're not that good and, in fact, we're a lot worse than we think we are.

A friend told me the story of a man travelling in a remote country who came on a sign that read, "Cannibal Cantina." The man was intrigued, so he went in, sat at a table, and picked up the menu. It read, "Fried missionary, $10; Boiled old tourist, $20; Grilled politician, $100." The man asked the waiter why the politician dish was so expensive. The waiter said, "Sir, have you ever tried to clean one of those suckers?"

It's not just politicians who don't clean up well. Nobody does, certainly not enough to present our goodness as an example of a sanctified Christian. Then what can we do? We do nothing. We just show up. We'll talk more about this in a later chapter, but for now it's important to understand the power of showing up. The power of our witness isn't in what we do but in who we are. In other words, if you are a Christian, you smell like Jesus and you can't help it. It's who you are.

I sometimes teach a seminary class on communicating to postmoderns. (I know that "postmodern" is an outdated word, but it does reflect a major change in our culture and it is still sometimes helpful to use it.) In the class we examine seventeen "marks" of postmodernity and all of them are bad and good at the same time. One of the things I tell students is that postmodernity is a gift to those who want to share Christ. "Before, nobody would listen unless

I knew more than they knew, had degrees they didn't have, and was an expert in ways they weren't. Our culture has changed. Now, not only do they not give a rip about those things, they're wary of them. Now I can say anything, go anywhere, talk to anyone, and get a hearing as long as I take my tie and mask off, set aside my agendas—both good and bad—and am willing to sit down and talk." I urge my students to try it and see if what I taught them was true. It's called "just showing up" without an agenda, a mask, a big black Bible, and an arrogant fix-it attitude. You can try it too. If you're willing to stop being so religious, you'll be surprised at what happens.

I have a friend whose improper sexual relationship with a married (but separated) man almost did her in. When she came to me, she was shocked by and devastated at her own behavior. She wept. I asked her what she was crying about. She told me her sin and said, "I've brought shame on the name of Christ, I've betrayed everything that is important to me, and I've destroyed any witness I could ever have."

"No," I said, "actually, you haven't. Why don't you go to that man and tell him what you just told me?"

After she told me that I was out of my mind, we talked more. She decided to do exactly what I suggested. She went to the man and told him that she needed to ask his forgiveness because she had been dishonest with him about who she was. She confessed to him what she had done (without mentioning his significant part in the sin) and repented with tears in his presence.

Want to know the rest of that story? After getting over his surprise, the man ended up becoming a Christian. He is even now walking with Christ.

Someone pointed out to me the way children will keep very still until they know they are safe. Have you ever noticed how, when a small child falls down and gets hurt, he maintains a kind of brief silence? When someone picks him up, perhaps a father, there is a time of quiet and then the screaming starts. We're like that. We remain in our silence, wear our masks, and plan our agendas of lies. We get hurt, and the only place we can scream is in the arms of a Father who is safe.

We've been talking about true truth. If you're a believer, every word here applies to you, without any "kickers" or "qualifiers." The Scripture says, "You are a chosen race, a royal priesthood, a holy nation, a people for his own possession . . ." (1 Peter 2:9). What the four doctrines in this chapter have given you are tools designed by God to allow us to show up. In fact, there is no way any of us can set aside our agendas and take off our masks until we find a place safe enough to do it. God is that safe place. You're forgiven, you're clothed, you're adopted, and you're sanctified. In the face of those truths, you now have a safe place . . . and his name is Jesus. You don't have to impress, manipulate, lie, or pretend anymore. I saw a bumper sticker not too long ago that read, "Jesus loves you. Everybody else thinks you're a pain." (Well, it didn't exactly say "pain," but this is a Christian book.) It's true, though—it doesn't matter what everybody else thinks about you. Why is that? The only one who counts is already crazy about you.

Am I suggesting that if we're willing to be that authentic (as authentic as my friend was to her lover) about who we are, what we've done and thought, and the one we belong to, that everybody we encounter will come to Christ? Of course not. But we've tried everything else and that hasn't worked.

At minimum, it can't hurt.

Behind the Mask

1. In your own words, describe justification, imputation, adoption, and sanctification. What does each mean to you personally?

2. What about your feelings in light of truth? Are they still important? Do they stand in the way of truth?

3. "Truth is true not because it works, but it works because it's true." Do you believe this? How is this "true" in your own life?

4. What does "getting better" look like to you? And how does it always start with the fact of who we are?

5. How does authenticity—taking off our masks and putting aside our hidden agendas—lead to our getting better?

Background Scriptures: 1 Timothy 3:15; Romans 5:1, 12–21; Romans 8:1–2; Galatians 4:3–7; 1 Corinthians 1:30–31; Hebrews 10:14; 1 Peter 2:9

Note to small group leaders: Refer to these Scriptures as needed during your discussion, along with Scripture passages in the chapter.

CHAPTER 9

When Hitting a Wall Feels Good

> Beloved, do not be surprised at the fiery trial when it
> comes upon you . . . as though something strange were
> happening to you. But rejoice . . . (1 Peter 4:12–13)

Let me give you a text and then remind you of a principle I
mentioned earlier. The text is Luke 12:2–3 where Jesus says,
"Nothing is covered up that will not be revealed, or hidden that will not be known. Therefore whatever you have
said in the dark shall be heard in the light, and what you
have whispered in private rooms shall be proclaimed on the
housetops."

Now the principle: There is a direct correlation between
a Christian's proclivity to wear a mask and God's proclivity
to rip it off.

Erik Guzman is the vice president of communications
at Key Life Network, the ministry of which I'm a part. A
few months ago his mother gave him a Christmas present
of a weekend retreat at the Monastery of the Holy Spirit

in Conyers, Georgia, one of my favorite places to visit. Monks built the chapel and it is breathtakingly beautiful. In fact, the wallpaper on my computer for years was a picture of that chapel taken from the back, looking at the altar. Erik had seen that photo, heard me talk about the monastery, and mentioned it to his mother. She decided that a great Christmas present would be a quiet weekend at the monastery.

So mother and son signed up for a weekend at the monastery. It wasn't what they expected. The monastery was sponsoring a retreat titled, "Good Grief." The people who had come for that retreat had faced horrible pain and were experiencing the grief that follows. Several were parents dealing with the suicide or death of their children. One lady's son had been murdered. Some had lost spouses to death. There were stories of abuse, loss, and sorrow.

"Steve," Erik told me, "the grief was so heavy you could cut it with a knife. They were looking for answers and there weren't any except the very obvious presence of Jesus, who had suffered everything they had suffered. Jesus identified with them. It didn't make the pain go away, but it made it doable. But the most amazing thing about the retreat was the absolute honesty. There weren't any masks—no pretending, no cover-up. People were in pain and their pain forced them to stand naked before God and their brothers and sisters. They couldn't do anything else."

They couldn't do anything else. That's it! It's called God taking away your options. I have a friend, Rob Beames, who recently wrote a book (from which I plan to quote a little later in this chapter), *Cornered by Grace*. That's what God does. He corners us . . . with his love and grace.

Before we go any further with what is going to be some difficult stuff, remember that it *is* God's grace. Charles

125

Spurgeon said that when it hurts, we should remember that God is too good to be cruel and too wise to be wrong. If that is true, when we can't trace his hand, we ought to trust his heart. Try to remember that as we look at a kind God who sometimes does unpleasant things in our lives. He is a merciful God who, in his mercy, rips off our masks and stomps on our hidden agendas.

A Kind God Allows Us to Suffer

A kind God allows us to suffer and, in taking away our "normal," forces us to be honest about who we are and where it hurts.

What Erik said about that retreat is absolutely true.

If you've never read the book of Job in the Bible but someone told you that it gives answers to the problem of suffering, that person lied to you. It's not a book of answers. It's a book of questions. Job did say in a burst of piety, "Though he slay me, I will hope in him" (Job 13:15). However that was the last spiritual thing he said. After that, Job commenced to "cuss and spit." In one place he tells God that he's had it and wants some answers to his questions. God's answers (Job 38—41) were more questions, questions designed to bring Job to the place where Job basically said, "Oops. Shut my mouth!" Not only did God confuse and shame Job, he hugged him and restored him, thereby affirming Job's honesty. God said in effect, "Good for you, Job. Finally you've taken off your mask. You really did good this time."

The problem of suffering (i.e., if God is sovereign and good, why is there suffering? He is either not good or not sovereign.) is not the subject of this book and there is so much more to be said about it than what I'm going to say here.[1] But ultimately, there is only one salient answer to the problem of our suffering: the suffering of Jesus as he identifies with our suffering.

Aside from that, let me tell you something about the suffering of the Christian. God is ripping off your mask and bringing you to the end of yourself. I had a heart attack a number of years ago and there is nothing that clarifies life better. I believe in "dying grace"—that when it is time for a Christian to die, he or she will have peace. In this case, I was scared spitless. Had I not been frightened, I really would have been scared. Do you know what happened because of the coronary? Throughout the process of healing, I became more authentic and honest in my teaching and preaching than I had ever been before. I suppose I still lie some, but I'm a lot better, because God made me get better by allowing me to go through the pain, the fear, and the trauma of a coronary.

You too. I don't know what you're going through right now or what those you love are facing. I don't want to sound flippant about your pain. I'm not. But it is good to remember that all things have a purpose (Romans 8:28) and one of God's purposes in the pain we endure is to rip off the mask so we can laugh and dance in his presence.

A Kind God Allows Us to Be Embarrassed

Not only will a kind God allow us to suffer, a kind God will also allow us to be embarrassed.

That's part of what Peter went through. Peter, in a burst of arrogance, responded to Jesus's prediction that all his disciples would run away at the prospect of Jesus's arrest and death with, "Maybe these other cowards, but not me" (Matthew 26). Shortly after that display of insufferable pride, Peter betrayed Jesus not just once, but three times. And then, Jesus brought it up at breakfast after the resurrection (John 21). Man, can you believe the embarrassment? Why? Jesus wanted to rip off Peter's mask and set him free.

A few years ago I spoke to a conference of the rich, powerful, and famous. It was a big deal and, frankly, I thought I was a big deal and that the folks who sponsored the conference had made a wise choice in choosing me. Do you know what happened? I made a fool of myself. No, it wasn't that I could see failure from where I was, that I made some mistakes in my presentation, that I could have made some corrections and improvements . . . I made a total and complete fool of myself.

And that wasn't the worst part. After my presentation I had to ride up to my room on the twenty-ninth floor on an elevator packed with people who had just seen me make a fool of myself. I've been doing this for a long time and have discovered that most of the time when the lecture bombed or the sermon didn't get to the first row, people will be kind and say, "That was interesting," or "I'll think about that a good deal." Even that didn't happen in the elevator. There was, other than an occasional cough or throat-clearing, total, absolute, and embarrassing silence. It was one of the longest elevator rides of my life.

When I finally got back to my room and locked the door, I knelt down by the bed and cried out to God. "How could you? At least you could have done it in my home church where people love me. Why did you do it to me in a place like this, with that many people I wanted to impress?" Other than the angels I heard laughing, I heard from him. He said he did it because he loved me. He was tired of my wearing the mask of "effective preacher," "articulate professor," and "wise guru." So he ripped it off. And I hated it.

You will too. When you say something so stupid that you can't believe you said it, when you wear the wrong dress or the ugly-looking tie and someone tells you, when you trip and fall in the wedding processional, and when you spill beer all over your new suit (you can add to the list), it's him! He's working to rip off the mask.

John DeBrine, a preacher and broadcaster friend of mine, told me about an incident that happened to a famous preacher. (John wouldn't tell me the name but he swears that it really happened.) This particular preacher realized when he got in front of his congregation that his zipper was down. Because his pulpit was clear Plexiglass, he couldn't remedy the situation without everybody seeing. Then he got an idea. The preacher moved over to where the large American flag was standing, pretended to straighten the flag, and at the same time, behind the flag, zipped up his zipper. The problem was that he inadvertently caught the flag in his zipper . . . and as he made his way back to the pulpit, the flag flew behind him the whole way.

That's funny. But more than that, it was God. If I had been in the congregation that day, I would have laughed. But I would have also sat at the feet of a preacher whose sermon was maybe the best sermon he had preached in a long time. It's hard to be pompous, godly, and self-righteous (all masks) when you've just embarrassed yourself by dragging the American flag across a stage in your zipper. That is God's love and grace in ripping the mask off.

A Kind God Allows Us to Be Wrong

But there's more. Not only will a kind and good God rip off your mask by allowing suffering and embarrassment because he loves you, he will also allow you to be wrong.

The Bible is replete with illustrations of God's people being dead wrong. Aside from Job and Peter, there is Paul who was wrong about Mark, Barnabas's cousin. Paul sent Mark home because of one mistake on the mission field and found out he was wrong (Colossians 4:10). Paul didn't remember that he followed a God of second, third, and fourth chances. And then there's Thomas, who was wrong about a dead man getting out of the grave (John 20), Peter who was wrong in siding with those who were angry at Paul and is called a "hypocrite" in Holy Writ (Galatians 2), and Apollos who had to be corrected by Priscilla and Aquila (Acts 18:26). It was good for all of them.

In a church I once served (this was in the "olden" days when things were done differently) I did a radical thing. I had the pulpit chair removed and sat in the congregation with my family, only coming to the chancel when I did my part of the service. I had singers and worship leaders do the same thing. It seemed to me appropriate symbolism for all of us to bring our gift before the God we all worshiped. I didn't think anybody would even notice, much less be upset.

Wrong.

Not only were some people upset, they got together a petition with a long list of names on it, demanding that I restore the pulpit chair and sit on it during the service. The petition suggested that the young people in the congregation needed a pastor who was an example of authority, some-one to look up to and respect. I don't handle those kinds of things very well and, in fact, tore up the petition and threw it into the trash can in front of the lady who brought it to me. (I know. I know. It wasn't exactly a sterling example of the fruit of the Spirit, but I was young. I'm better now . . . at least some.) I didn't say it to the lady but probably should have said, "You don't understand. The last thing the young people in this church need is someone who speaks from Sinai. What they need is someone who knows that God doesn't take lightly anybody who worships at any altar but his own." But there was more to it than that. I knew, even then, that God would rip off a mask of authority, power, and expertise if I wore it.

In the introduction to this book, I confessed my phoniness to you. I also suggested that all Christian writers of Christian books should confess their sins in the first chapter of their books. Then we would listen to them. I wasn't trying to be cute. I was being wise. I know that God delights in ripping off the masks of those who pretend to have all the answers to all the questions.

I used to stay up at night, worried about question-and-answer sessions in the conferences where I would speak or teach. Do you know why? I was afraid I wouldn't have an answer and, when I kept talking until something came to mind, people would see the scam. I don't worry about that anymore. (I have confessed my sins to you, so cut me a bit of slack when I brag a bit.) In fact, I'm not bothered at all by any questions for which I don't have answers. It's quite freeing to say, as I heard R. C. Sproul once say, "Lady, I have a great answer for you. I don't know." It doesn't bother me to be wrong anymore and I'm free. In fact, I've taken to saying at the end of some sermons I preach, "Half of what I just taught you is wrong. The problem is that I don't know which half. So you're going to have to get your Bibles and do some checking."

That drives people nuts, but it pleases God. It saves him the trouble of having to rip off the mask of one of his servants in order to make him free.

A Kind God Allows Us to Sin . . . and Sometimes Sin Big

There is one more thing that a kind God will do to rip off the mask. A kind God will allow you to sin . . . and sometimes sin big.

Well, maybe it would be better to say that a kind God will clearly reveal your sin to you or he will clearly reveal it to others. He will reveal the greatness of your sin to you or allow you to sin greatly. It's less painful when he shows you and, because he loves you, doesn't tell everybody else.

The public revelation of one's sins is not pretty. Case in point: The time Nathan confronted David about his murder and adultery. Go read 2 Samuel 12. If that doesn't make you wince, there's something wrong with you. David's sin was horrible and he deserved no compassion, but it's difficult not to feel a little sorry for him as he goes through that awful public humiliation. And yet it is from that public humiliation that David writes one of the most profound confessions found in the entire Bible, Psalm 51:

> Have mercy on me, O God,
>   according to your steadfast love;
> according to your abundant mercy
>   blot out my transgressions . . .
>
> For I know my transgressions,
>   and my sin is ever before me . . .

Go read that psalm; its profound confession before a holy God will move you deeply. There you will find no self-justification ("What else could I do?"), no list of mitigating circumstances (e.g., "I was drunk and didn't know what I was doing"), no excuses ("I was tired with the burdens of government"), and no spinning ("Uriah was a pain in the posterior, and Bathsheba wanted me as much as I wanted her"). Read that psalm and watch God ripping the mask off David. It will give hope to the great sinner (that would be you and me) that God is a gracious and forgiving God. And not only that, you will know the source of David's power, the reason he could write such incredible and moving psalms, and why he is called "a man after [God's] own heart" (1 Samuel 13:14).

In a previous book I wrote something for which I've received a lot of criticism. Sometimes I wish I had never written it. Nevertheless, I'm going to say it again. (Stupid is forever.) The greatest gift that God gives to the people he loves is their sin . . . *when they know it*. And the greatest curse to a Christian is that Christian's obedience . . . *when he or she knows it*. Let me tell you what I mean.

I'm often accused of being antinomian (a word coined by Martin Luther which means that sin doesn't matter) and encouraging people to sin. Most of the accusations leveled at me are accurate but this one is just not true. In fact, it is just the opposite. As I understand it, the Bible teaches that people are sinners because we sin . . . all of us. I refuse to take credit for your sin. You were doing fine with it before I ever came along. You were sinning before you ever even heard of me, and the only reason you know my name is because someone gave you this book or you came across it by accident. I had nothing to do with your sin. It's not your mother, or your brother, or me. It's you.

But more important, sin, rebellion, and disobedience have infiltrated the fiber of every bit of God's creation and all of God's creatures. That's not because God likes sin. He hates sin because it is destructive and dangerous to everything that is important. It isn't because God doesn't want us to have a good time. He is not the "spoilsport" some preachers and religious folks make him out to be. It isn't because he takes delight in punishing us when we get out of line. Good heavens, God did just the opposite and perpetrated the greatest injustice in the history of the world, the punishment poured out on his own Son as a "propitiation for our sins" (1 John 2:2).

God allowed sin for his grandeur and majesty (the Bible calls that his "glory") and for your freedom. For God's sake, don't waste your sin; acknowledge it. Don't kick against the goads, carefully plan your agendas of protection, or tighten the masks lest anyone see. Besides, God, because he loves you, won't let you do it. Then you will be free.

I mentioned my friend Rob Beames's book, *Cornered by Grace: Right Where You Need to Be*. In that book, Rob said that for seven years he worked in an environment where he was free—free to experiment with computer software. He was learning, and nobody expected much from him, so he could try a lot of new things, click around wherever he wanted, and had no apprehension that he would hurt anything that couldn't be fixed. Then, he said, in an effort to increase his skills, he took on a new challenge. Rob knew this wasn't a place where he was as free, but he also knew he could handle it. At first, things went as expected. "That all changed one day," Rob said, "as I was trying to modify a report. Within the hour, I found out that I had impacted hundreds of people across the company with an invalid script that crashed the server. Had I been in a test environment, I could have avoided this catastrophe . . . but the deed was already done, not only to all those who weren't able to use the application for an hour, but also to my own psyche."

Rob said that everything changed. For a while, he didn't want to learn anything new because he was afraid of what might happen. He was afraid of losing his job, and his fear of crashing the server made him hesitate before doing the simplest thing.

"Unfortunately," Rob wrote, "this is the culture in which many Christians live for a large part of their lives. We often try to live out our faith afraid to do anything for God because we fear it's all going to crash down on us if we mess up. Not only does it stifle the joy that God desires for us, it also debilitates the effectiveness of our witness. When unbelievers observe us living in the fear of failure, worried about the punishment we might incur, how attractive is our message of freedom? It's not very desirable at all. Most everyone already has that kind of pressure. Who needs any more of that?"[2]

That's it. God hates the way the shame, fear, and guilt of our hidden agendas and masks rob us of freedom and joy. He hated it so much that he went through a "mess" of trouble and pain to set us free. You've probably heard some worship leader or preacher say, "He loves you and me just the way we are but he loves us too much to leave us there." If you're like me (i.e., neurotic), you read into that statement (and it may even have been intended that way) that you had to give up smoking, be nicer, and stop sinning. The statement is true but it's not what you think.

I have a friend who told me that she had seen a billboard advertising Harley-Davidson motorcycles. In big, bold letters, the billboard shouted to those who were driving by, "Hey, you in the cage!" That's what God says to us about our masks and agendas. "Hey, you in the cage! I love you . . . and I'm going to get you out." After you have suffered enough, been embarrassed enough, been wrong enough, and sinned enough, he will hug you and invite you to a party he throws for people who are really free, who don't care much what others think, and who have been deeply loved when they didn't deserve it.

You'll be better for it.

I know, I know. I hate it when people say that to me. But in this case, it's true. Maybe not "better" but free—and that really is better.

Behind the Mask

1. Do you really believe that a kind God allows you to suffer, to be embarrassed, to be wrong, and to sin? Why or why not?

2. What do you think of the principle, "There is a direct correlation between a Christian's proclivity to wear a mask and God's proclivity to rip it off"? Have you found this to be true in your own life?

3. Why would God "reveal the greatness of your sin to you or allow you to sin greatly"? What purpose does this serve?

4. "The greatest gift that God gives to the people he loves is their sin . . . *when they know it*. And the greatest curse to a Christian is that Christian's obedience . . . *when he or she knows it*." What does this mean? Give an example.

Background Scriptures: 1 Peter 4:12–13; Luke 12:2–3; Romans 8:28; Psalm 51

Note to small group leaders: Refer to these Scriptures as needed during your discussion, along with Scripture passages in the chapter.

CHAPTER 10

Therefore

There is therefore now no condemnation for those who are in Christ Jesus. (Romans 8:1)

I teach preaching to seminary students. I remember the first class I taught years ago. I had been asked to fly up from Miami (where Key Life was located at the time) to Orlando (where the seminary is located) each week to teach the course. My first lecture was probably different from most preaching courses. "I don't want to be here," I said to that class as they became very quiet. "I don't have the time to do this and I don't need this job. I am not your mother and I don't want to be your friend. I'm here for one reason. You don't know how to talk. If you listen and learn, I'll teach you. If you don't, you won't. Now let's get to it."

I must say that shortly after I made that statement, I repented of it. I got seminary students on my heart and learned to love them. I did, in fact, become their friend and, in some cases, their mother. But I did teach them how to talk. Not only do I teach seminary students how to talk, I wrote a book on the subject (*How to Talk So People Will Listen*). Let me give you the essence of what I teach seminary students and what I wrote in that book, and save you some money. I taught and wrote that the most important thing about communication is to ask the question, "So what?" In other words, it doesn't matter what you preach if it doesn't matter what you preach.

If you've listened to Bible teachers very much, you've probably heard them say when they come to a verse with the word "therefore" in it, something like, "Whenever you see the word 'therefore' in the Bible, it is appropriate to ask, what is the 'therefore' there for?"

That's what we're going to do in what follows. It's the "therefore" of all that I've written up to this point. I gave you a lot of Scripture and a lot of propositional truth. Now let's get to, as it were, the "therefore."

Therefore You're Safe

Frankly, there aren't many safe places in the world physically or emotionally. From the battlefields of the Mideast to the violence in the most protected American neighborhoods, it is wise to be very careful. Maybe one should even carry a gun.

(I know. I know. Christians aren't supposed to carry guns and that's true when serving Christ. In fact, when we are persecuted for our faith, we are called to just take it while turning the other cheek. However, in the case of random violence, you can shoot those suckers. So a gun might be in order.)

In trying to deal with our agendas and masks, emotional safety is hard to come by too. I don't think there has ever been a time when our culture was more uptight, critical, and condemning than it is now. When one combines the political correctness of the popular, "in" narrative of our culture with the natural human default position of self-righteousness, we live in a very difficult and anxiety-ridden time.

A number of years ago I was asked to write a chapter in a book published in honor of my friend John Frame. He is one of the brightest theological minds of our time and maybe the most kind and gentle friend I have. I was at a meeting once where John was lecturing. During the question-and-answer time, he was asked a very controversial question. He began his insightful comments with, "Oh dear . . ." After the meeting was over, I went to him and said, "Dr. Frame, you are a revolutionary. You say things that all of us think but are afraid to say. But listen to me. Revolutionaries don't say 'Oh dear.' If you want me to teach you how to cuss, I will, but don't say 'Oh dear' anymore, okay?" It was a joke but John wasn't sure and I think he considered (before I started laughing) taking me up on my offer.

As I prepared to write the chapter honoring John Frame, I read a pile of comments about him online and in some books. To my horror I found the most angry, harsh, self-righteous, critical, and demeaning material about John that you can imagine. I was shocked and saddened by it, and addressed the issue in the chapter I wrote. The horrible things that were said about John came from "Christians" who made unbelievers sound like sweet, elderly ladies serving cookies. If you haven't encountered that sort of thing in Christian circles, you probably haven't been paying attention. It's everywhere and it's a major reason for our fear of letting people know who we really are, what we really think, and how we really live our lives.

But here's the important thing. In that kind of atmosphere, if our "safe place" doesn't come from somewhere other than the secular culture in general and the Christian culture in particular, we will always hide, lie, and pretend. We will never be free of our efforts to play-act. And because we're not free, we will be miserable, afraid, lonely, and marginalized in our relationships.

Many years ago when I wrote my first book, Dr. Addison Leitch, who was then academic dean at Gordon-Conwell Seminary, read it, liked it, and wrote some kind things about it. Not only that, he invited me to visit him. After that visit, Dr. Leitch and I became friends and, frankly, I was overwhelmed that he wanted to be my friend, to have meals together, and to spend time with me. It was a gift that I highly valued.

After my first visit with Dr. Leitch, I drove back to the church I was serving on the South Shore near Boston. When I walked into my study, there was a man waiting for me. He wasn't happy. In fact, he was there to criticize me for something I had said and done. I don't even remember what it was all about or even the man's name, but I do remember thinking as he leveled his verbal gun, *You can say whatever you want. Dr. Addison Leitch likes me and I don't care whether you do or not.*

It's hard to keep from wearing a mask to please the people you want to please—unless, of course, there is someone really valuable to you who is already pleased. That would be Jesus.

I have some good news, and it's from a safe place beyond what others think, beyond the places where our culture tries to mold us, and beyond the harsh cries of the con men and the lies of the sellers of trinkets. What they think is of far less importance than you think. The good news is from Jesus: "Let not your hearts be troubled. Believe in God; believe also in me" (John 14:1). What does that mean?

In the context of the John 14 passage, Jesus is talking about eternity and the place he has prepared, but even in the context of the places where we live, work, and play on earth, those words are powerful. No matter what anybody says, no matter what false teachers teach, and no matter what our neurotic guilt lays on us, there is the voice of the only one who knows and who is clear: "Therefore, I tell you, do not be anxious about your life. . . . Look at the birds of the air. . . . Are you not of more value than they? . . . your heavenly Father knows . . . But seek first the kingdom of God and his righteousness . . ." (Matthew 6:25–26, 32–33). Jesus said that there was no greater love than the love of one who would lay down his life for his friends and "you are my friends" (John 15:13–14).

We've talked about imputation, where God has put the righteousness of Christ into our account. The answer to the "So what?" question is this: You've got a friend in high places. He will never say, "I've had it with you," and he will never leave us alone in the dark. He is quite fond of us and that gives us the freedom to say, "I don't care what you think or say about me. The only one who counts thinks I'm valuable, acceptable, and righteous." In that safe place we are free to rip off our masks and "stomp those suckers flat."

Therefore You're Real

One of my favorite books is C. S. Lewis's *The Great Divorce*. It is a story showing that the closer one gets to the deep mountains of God/heaven, the more real one becomes; the further away one runs, the less real. It is a profound commentary on heaven and hell, and reflects Lewis's belief that hell is locked from the inside. But the book also reflects a reality for those of us who are dealing with our masks. The closer one gets to God, the less one feels the need for a mask or a hidden agenda. In other words, the closer one gets to the "real" God, the more "real" one becomes oneself.

My late mentor, Fred Smith, had a close friend who was dying. Fred's friend decided that he needed help in dying, so he called in a number of his friends. He called them his "death board" and they were charged with overseeing his death. One was a doctor because Fred's friend said he wanted to know what was going on medically as he faced death. Another was a lawyer because he wanted him to oversee the legal issues of his will and the repercussions of his death. He also appointed a pastor to speak to his spiritual needs and a counselor to help him deal with his fear of death. As Fred listened to his friend's commissions to his "board," he noticed that his dying friend had not given him a job. "Okay," Fred said, "this is good stuff, but you haven't told me what I'm here for. What do you want me to do?" "Fred," the dying man said, "your job is to be a BS filter."

That's what the Holy Spirit is. The more we walk with Christ, the more the Holy Spirit tells us what is true and what isn't, what is a lie and what is the truth, and what is nonsense and what is important and real. Jesus called the Holy Spirit "the Spirit of truth" (John 14:17) and said that the Spirit "will guide you into all the truth" (John 16:13). The Spirit of God has a job and his job is to make us real.

In an article in *First Things*, George Weigel wrote about the diplomacy of John Paul II and the seven lessons we can learn from him. The seventh lesson is that media reality isn't necessarily reality. He writes,

> The problem of confusing reality with "media reality" or narrative has intensified since 1979, in no small part because of the ubiquity of social media and instant internet commentary, both of which readily

create narratives that seem to be reality. Yet the statesmen of the twenty-first century would do well to take a lesson from John Paul II and read the "signs of the times" with their own eyes, rather than through lenses befogged by media-generated narratives. The same lesson applies to churchmen. Church leaders, clerical and lay, who respond to media-generated narratives about the Catholic Church rather than to the imperatives of the Gospel are not going to advance either the evangelical mission of the Church or the cause of human dignity and freedom. The Gospel has power, and its power can cut through the densest of false narratives.[1]

When Christians learn to identify their false masks and hidden agendas, something really exciting happens: there is a BS filter about everything around them.

Did you hear about the new believer who found Christ in a Texas church where they believed in entire sanctification (total perfection) after one's baptism? After this particular man was saved, he insisted on being baptized even though it was winter and the river where the baptisms were normally performed was frozen over. At his insistence, the church leaders went down to the river and chiseled out a hole in the ice, and the pastor baptized the man. When the man came up shivering out of the icy water, he shouted, "Praise God! Praise God! I'm sanctified! It's so wonderful that I'm not even cold." "We have to do it again," the pastor said through clenched teeth. "He's lying."

That's what the Holy Spirit does for Christians as we make our way through the minefields of the world. When commercials promise us something they can't deliver, when politicians knowingly mislead us, when a preacher tells us that Christ's work isn't finished and sufficient, and when

143

we fall prey to our own neurotic fears, the Holy Spirit says, "He's lying!"

For our purposes here, when we pretend to be something we're not, condemn others for their lack of faithfulness when our unfaithfulness is greater than theirs, when we say we're fine when we're not, when we deny the reality of who we really are, the Holy Spirit whispers, "You're lying." Eventually (and it is a slow process sometimes) we listen and become more and more real. The masks become a cumbersome burden and the hidden agendas are no longer worth the effort.

Here's a question hardly anybody asks. They don't ask it for the same reason we bury people in their best clothes surrounded by flowers. We do it because we don't want to think that—in a beautiful casket surrounded by flowers and dressed like he or she is going to the prom—there is a cold, dead corpse. The question is this: What matters when you're the corpse? Probably the most important answer to that question is that unreal masks, hidden and dishonest agendas, and being accepted by people who are also going to end up in a casket—none of it matters. In fact, it's all about as valuable as a bag of chicken feed.

Therefore You Can Look in the Mirror Without Blushing

David Tyra is the pastor of First Baptist Church of Linton, Indiana, and a gifted musician. We've been friends forever. I love David for a lot of reasons but the main reason is the reality of his walk with Christ. The other day David shared with me (we share with each other some things neither of us would share with most people) something he had written in his journal while studying Deuteronomy 3:23–28. In that passage Moses is quite irritated with God and

144

tells him so. God has not let him see the Promised Land, for which Moses has given his life and efforts for a whole lot of years. As David read that passage, he thought that he was like Moses. David has worked (as have most pastors) for a lot of years as the pastor of his church. He'd always hoped (as every pastor worth his salt hopes) that the church would grow and a lot more people would worship there.

I always felt that way too. "Lord," I would sometimes say, "what am I—chopped liver? I've been working here all these years. And then there's this pastor down the street who's put up a tent and already has 10,000 people. I love you as much as he does and, frankly, I preach better. What's wrong with me?"

I know, I know . . . and I repent. David too.

David reluctantly gave me permission to share some of his thoughts on that passage in Deuteronomy. His people love him in profound ways. They know that they have a pastor who "smells like Jesus" and they are quite affirming of his loving ministry to them. But still David was feeling down because he didn't see the fruit of his ministry—the fruit he had hoped to see:

> I have wanted to preach to a great and growing church (or alternatively), to play and sing to great and growing crowds of people. You have denied me these things and I confess that I have not been satisfied with your decision. I believe and must proceed under the assumption that this is your will for me and, by your grace, I humble myself before you and accept your righteous judgment in this matter.
>
> My part is still important, isn't it, Lord? I'm to minister to these people, feed them, build them up, and encourage them with your Word, the gospel of

your grace . . . to prepare them for their trials, and get them ready to die. These are needful and important things and, while I didn't choose them, I accept the place where you've called me. I surrender to you, *Abba*.

When I read what David wrote, I think I heard the angels sing. His preaching is profound and his music quite moving because he has looked in the mirror and faced the reality of who he is, his sin, and his failure. And when he did, he was hugged.

Let me give you a truth so apparent that I hate to even mention it. A Christian will never be real to others until he or she is real with himself or herself. You've heard the statement that before a con man can con others, he must first con himself. That's true and Christians do a lot of that. Frankly, I can't explain why so many of us (myself included) are so critical of others when we are so very uncritical of ourselves about the same issues. When we do that, we rob ourselves of one of the great gifts we have been given.

Jesus said, "Judge not, that you be not judged. . . . Why do you see the speck that is in your brother's eye, but do not notice the log that is in your own eye? Or how can you say to your brother, 'Let me take the speck out of your eye,' when there is the log in your own eye?" (Matthew 7:1–4). Stand before a mirror and remember what Jesus said. Then confess it and feel the joy.

I have a friend who is, even as I write this, discovering some of his "lost memories." He's a trained psychologist so his efforts are not uninformed. He keeps getting flashes of painful memories and is trying to put the pieces together in the puzzle of his childhood. He will often tell me what he's discovering and will sometimes say that he is frightened.

But, in his finer moments, he is "kissing the demons" of his own life and those demons are, as a result, losing their power. In the same way, we have to "kiss the demons" with which we struggle. That's hard to do unless there is a safe place to do it.

That's the "therefore" of the Christian. I've been to the confessional and I've been loved and accepted. I've found that I can say anything and won't be kicked out. That is an incredible gift Jesus gave us. The problem is that most of us don't take advantage of that gift. I have a friend whose daughter had a puppy she loved. The puppy was lost and, despite the family's efforts, he was never found. In her grief, the daughter told her father, "I told him stuff I never told anybody."

If you should stumble on me early in the morning when I'm praying, you would be surprised. You would be surprised by my "cussing and spitting" (the psalmist gave me permission to do that), my complaining, and the times I tell God that I disagree (as in "Lord, you don't love them. If you loved them, you wouldn't treat them that way"). You would be surprised by the silence and sometimes even the laughter. But what would really surprise you would be my confession of sin. It often has a prominent place in my time with him. Not only that, it is sometimes very long.

I love to confess and repent—really love it. I'm neurotic but not about this. Martin Luther once told a colleague that he ought to go out and sin so he would have something to confess. Luther knew a secret that I know too: confession and repentance are not chores to me. Instead, they have become a delight. It is the one place where I feel loved, and in ways that I simply can't feel when I've "done good."

Years ago, I got a critical letter from a man heavily involved in the national gay and lesbian movement. He was angry because I had said some things with which he strongly disagreed. He was a Christian and, subsequent to that letter, we became friends. In our conversation, I told him that he was missing one of the delights of being a Christian, and that was being hugged. "My sins," I said, "are greater than your sins. I'm so screwed up that I don't throw many rocks at others. But the difference between you and me is that you never get hugged because you don't think you need it."

I must confess, though, that confession and repentance weren't always that easy. I wanted to lay out my case (the way Job did) before God and explain. I would tell God about what those "horrible people" had done to me and said about me. I wanted to tell him "what really happened," thinking he would understand my sin if only he knew the whole story. I put on a mask and told him that he knew my heart and how pure it was. I still do that sometimes. But when it was the central methodology of my prayer life, do you know how God reacted to my prayers? He reacted with silence. It wasn't an unloving silence. On occasion I even felt his compassion. I never felt rejection or dismissed . . . but I didn't get hugged. Now I've gotten better because I got worse—or at least I got better because I was willing to face the worst.

Now when I pray, "Search me, O God, and know my heart! Try me and know my thoughts! And see if there be any grievous way in me, and lead me in the way everlasting!"(Psalm 139:23–24), it isn't a negative and fearful thing. In effect, it's saying to God, "Let's look at my life so I can find a place where you can forgive me and love me more." And no, it doesn't make me sin more. This is a methodology (a biblical one) where most of the time I sin less. I sin less and see more, and I suspect that I'll never run out of places to get hugged until I get Home and I'm just like Jesus. Then the love will be experienced 100 percent of the time.

Frederick Buechner says, "It is important to tell at least from time to time the secret of who we truly and fully are— *even if we tell it only to ourselves* [italics mine]—because otherwise we run the risk of losing track of who we truly and fully are and little by little come to accept instead the highly edited version which we put forth in hope that the world will find it more acceptable than the real thing."[2]

Therefore I'm Dangerous

Let me confess something to you. You scare me to death. I've written a lot of books and, frankly, some of those books aren't that good. Shortly after what I'm writing here is published, the reviews will start coming in. And then the sales figures will be given to me. Then my friends will start saying what they really think about what I wrote. Finally, you'll read it and may even let me know what you think. That's scares the spit out of me. I desperately want you to like me and what I wrote. I want you to think that all the work I put into this book was worthwhile. I don't want you to see the places where I'm unsure of what I've written, that required ten editors to straighten out the original manuscript, and where I asked myself, "Is this really true?" In fact, I might not even let this book be published.

But what if "perfect love casts out fear" (1 John 4:18)? What if I'm perfectly loved no matter what I've done or where I've been? What if God accepts me just as I am as long as I'm willing to face, with him, who I really am? What if I get free of pretending? What would happen then? I'll tell you what would happen. I would be really dangerous.

I sometimes grow tired of "nice" Christians and even find it irritating when I'm "nice." The reason the people in the Bible are dangerous isn't because they were good, and courageous and strong because of it. They weren't "in the face" of the world because they were right all the time. They weren't a powerful adversary because, as someone said, they "out-thought, out-lived and out-died" everybody else. Do you know what made them dangerous? They were dangerous because they knew they were loved, accepted, and sent by a God who would never leave them. When one looks at the biblical witness, it is a list of very human, sinful, and wrong people . . . people who, though they were "stiff-necked" (Exodus 32:9), belonged to God. They lived, spoke, loved, and stood in that knowledge, and it made them dangerous.

By the time we start reading the New Testament and see what God was up to, we are overwhelmed by the power and impact of the early church. They said what needed to be said to the people who needed to hear it. They died when it was necessary to die for those who needed to see someone willing to die for truth. They faced any obstacle, climbed any mountain, and went to any country to live and speak truth. They didn't care. And they were dangerous. "These men who have turned the world upside down have come here also" (Acts 17:6).

In a while, we'll talk about family matters—how hidden agendas and masks cripple the witness of God's people. But for now, if we Christians ever get honest about ourselves, who we are, and what God's grace really means, we will be dangerous.

We should say to the world, "Be afraid. Be very afraid."

Behind the Mask

1. Where is your "safe place"? How does it free you from the need to hide, lie, and pretend?
2. Do you find that the closer you are to the "real" God, the more "real" you become? What does the "real you" look like?
3. What matters when you're the corpse?
4. "A Christian will never be real to others until he or she is real with himself or herself." Is this true in your own experience?
5. Once you're loved, accepted, and free, you're dangerous. What does that look like?

Background Scriptures: Romans 8:1; John 14; Matthew 6; Matthew 7:1–4; Psalm 139:23–24

Note to small group leaders: Refer to these Scriptures as needed during your discussion, along with Scripture passages in the chapter.

CHAPTER 11

Family Secrets

You have set our iniquities before you, our secret sins in the light of your presence. (Psalm 90:8)

The late Bruce Thielemann was my friend and one of the most gifted preachers I've ever heard. Bruce was the pastor of First Presbyterian Church in Pittsburgh and, at the end of his life, the dean of the chapel at Grove City College. Before coming to Pennsylvania, Bruce had been the pastor of Glendale Presbyterian Church in California. While Bruce was there, he told me he went through a very dark period of discouragement. He was a lifelong bachelor and had just come back from a speaking trip to Africa. The evening he got back to his high-rise apartment, he said that he stood at the window looking out at the city, and was overwhelmed by his loneliness, depression, and discouragement.

Bruce said that he got his contact list and started calling pastor friends in the city. He told them that he desperately needed a friend, someone to talk to. Each of the pastors said they would love to meet with him but, when they got out their calendars, none of them could do it for at least a week. With some, it would take even longer. When Bruce got to the last name in his book of contacts, his pastor friend said, "Bruce, I will be glad to meet with you but right now my schedule is so heavy. Could we meet in a couple of weeks?" "No," Bruce replied. "I need to talk to someone yesterday and you're my last hope. I'm in serious trouble and I'm simply not going to let you blow me off. Could you meet me tomorrow for lunch, please?" The pastor reluctantly agreed and they met in a restaurant in a Glendale suburb. When they had ordered, Bruce poured his heart out about his loneliness, depression, and discouragement. When he finished, his pastor friend said, "Bruce, do you know why I didn't want to meet with you? Last night I came home and found my wife in the arms of another man." Bruce said that if I had been there that day, I would have seen two pastors holding hands and crying together.

Sometimes I think about Bruce and the pastor in that restaurant, holding hands and crying together. I think that, if I were an artist, I would paint a picture of it. I would include in the painting angels surrounding the table where they ate and Jesus sort of off to the side, smiling. That day in that restaurant, those two guys "did church."

A friend who visited the opening of Disney World in Orlando said to a Disney official that it was a shame Walt Disney didn't live to see it all. The official said, "Don't worry, he did. If he had not seen it before it happened, it never would have happened." Let's envision the church and what it could be before we get there.

Have you ever noticed what the New Testament says about the church . . . and how often we don't even come close to living up to what the Bible says we should do and be? Do you know why that's so? It's because God wants us to see the picture and keep looking at it so that more and more, little by little, bit by bit, we become the reality of what the picture has shown us.

When Paul wrote to the Galatians, one sees the frustration he felt: "O foolish Galatians! . . . Did you receive the Spirit by works of the law or by hearing with faith?" (Galatians 3:1–2). Jesus reflected a similar frustration: "O faithless generation, how long am I to be with you?" (Mark 9:19). John wrote to the people in his church, "I am writing to you, little children, because your sins are forgiven for his name's sake [yeah, but he had to keep reminding them]. I am writing to you, fathers, because you know him who is from the beginning [most the time]. I am writing to you, young men, because you have overcome the evil one [but it doesn't look like it sometimes]. . . . I write to you, young men, because you are strong [occasionally], and the word of God abides in you [in your finer moments], and you have overcome the evil one [yes and no]" (1 John 2:12–14). John wrote that, not because it was a daily reality, but because he had a picture from God of the way things ought to be. Just read the great love passage of 1 Corinthians 13. If you live up to that kind of love, you will get the next vacancy in the Trinity.

So why bring it up? God knows us, we haven't surprised him, and he knew how far away we would wander from the picture he gave us. You see, God wants us to envision the way it ought to be, to face the fact that it isn't that way at all, and to put us on a path to make the vision the reality. Someone said about individual Christians that God gives us a mirror and a picture of Jesus. In the mirror we see who we are now and in the picture we see who we're going to be.

He promised, "What we will be has not yet appeared; but we know that when he appears we will be like him" (1 John 3:2). I think that's true and it's also true about the church.

One often hears some well-meaning Christian say that we need to return to the early church and model ourselves after them. That sounds good until one starts reading the New Testament. They were as screwed up as we are, fought even more than we do, and were sinners who sinned maybe even more than we sin. However, there is something to the "finer moments" of the early church that we must not miss. It's not what you think. Those finer moments aren't given to us to make us feel guilty or to beat us over the head because we don't even come close. God gave us a picture of what this thing is all about. It's about being forgiven, free, and absolutely captivated by the incredible power of God's love. It's a picture of Jesus loving the whores and the drunks, the Pharisees and the pagans, and the self-righteous and the ones who don't even know what righteousness is. It's a picture of wounded, bleeding, and sinful Christians making the world different because they are in it.

In another chapter down the line, we'll consider the implications that burning masks and shredding agendas have for the mission of the church. But first I want to show you the picture God gave us of what church really looks like. It's not what we are but it is where we could be moving. Do I think we'll achieve the reality behind the picture? Are you crazy? Of course not! I've already told you that I'm cynical, and you should know that the positive side of cynicism is realism. I've been doing this for a very long time and I'm shocked by very little that happens in the church or in me. I have very few expectations. However, I do have some and I would like to share some of them with you.

What would happen if, little by little, we allowed Jesus to help us deal with our shame?

The Old Testament has a good deal to say about shame. Isaiah wrote that God's own "shall not be put to shame . . . to all eternity" (Isaiah 45:17). To make sure we got it, Isaiah says it again in Isaiah 49:23, "Those who wait for me [God] shall not be put to shame." And then there is Joel's prophecy that "it shall come to pass afterward, that I will pour out my Spirit on all flesh; your sons and your daughters shall prophesy, your old men shall dream dreams, and your young men shall see visions" and God's people "shall never again be put to shame" (Joel 2:27–28). Over and over again, the Psalms refer to God's people not being shamed.

Almost always in the Old Testament, shame is connected to divine retribution and reward on earth. For instance, in Psalm 119:6, the psalmist says that because he has his eye "fixed on all your [God's] commandments" [and, of course, is obedient to them], he "shall not be put to shame." In other words, a lack of shame is the reward one gets for doing the right thing. That reward involves acceptance, praise, glory, riches, health, and favor. Even in the book of Job, the basic thrust of Job's problem is that he is publicly shamed, and his friends (the ones he has left) keep telling him that he was getting what he deserved. Do it right and it will come out right.

All of the teaching in the Old Testament is, of course, true. You really will not have to be shamed if you do it right. The "fly in the ointment" is a big one, though: There is no way that we have ever, are now, or ever will do it right. Not only that, the fact that we don't do it right is the reason we create masks to suggest that we *are* doing it right. It's the reason we manufacture hidden agendas to plan our lives so that we can foster the lie. Do you think God knew that? Of course he knew. And if he knew, why in the world would he tell us to fix our shame by doing it right? Is God a sadist? Does he delight in dangling the hope in front of us and taking it away when we reach for it?

I've been teaching Romans on one of our syndicated radio broadcasts (*Key Life*) for the last few months and I'll probably still be teaching it until Jesus comes back. I really didn't think it would take as long as it appears it will take. But the more I get into Romans, the more I realize that almost the entire book is dealing with shame. While the word "shame" isn't used very often, the reality is everywhere. Paul does, in Romans 9:33 and Romans 10:11, quote Isaiah, who said anybody who believed in God wouldn't be put to shame, but the entire book is an amazing and wonderful open door to living a shame-free life—a life where one doesn't have to pretend to be something one isn't, where play-acting is no longer necessary, and where we move toward obtaining "the freedom of the glory of the children of God" (Romans 8:21).

Shame-based people are always afraid that people are going to find out how bad they are. They live in constant fear of making fools of themselves and then being rejected. If their clothes aren't exactly right, their house isn't neat, their lives not upstanding and Christian, their children not perfect, their marriage not a witness, and their religion not lived properly, there is hidden shame. What if someone finds out? What if people knew the truth? What if I'm rejected, kicked out of the church, not invited to the party, ignored, or marginalized because of it? What if nobody will love me? It's a horrible place to live.

Here's the important thing and the key to a remedy: Everybody lives there! People are my business and I know.

Besides that, as I've shown you in this book, "the Bible tells me so." I live there and you do too. There isn't a single person who doesn't, to one degree or another, live in a house of shame. You know those people who are very spiritual and really walk the talk? The preacher who seems to have a hotline to God and is better than the cretins who sit in the pews? The lady who teaches the Bible and wants people to follow her example of goodness and godliness? The man who disciples others and loves to "show them how" to follow Christ? The radio teacher with the deep voice who sounds so sure of himself that you're certain he doesn't ever doubt, sin, or wonder what the sand he's doing?

It's all a lie. Every bit of it.

In the last book Brennan Manning wrote before he died, his normal honest and in-your-face transparency was on steroids: "Warning: Mine has been anything but a straight shot, more like a crooked path filled with thorns and crows and vodka. Prone to wander? You bet. I've been a priest, then an ex-priest. Husband, then ex-husband. Amazed crowds one night and lied to friends the next. Drunk for years, sober for a season, then drunk again. I've been John the beloved, Peter the coward, and Thomas the doubter all before the waitress brought the check. I've shattered every one of the Ten Commandments six times Tuesday. And if you believe that the last sentence was for dramatic effect, it wasn't."[1]

I got an email from a young friend this morning. He sent me his bio and wanted my opinion since, he said, I was partly responsible for the "out of the box" nature of what he had written. His name is Chris Pearce and the fact that he gave me permission to use his name suggests that he's the "real deal" and is moving out of his house of shame. In fact, when I asked him for permission to use what he had written, he wrote back, "Tears of joy and grace here. Of course you can use it. The freedom comes from keeping the closet open so the skeletons can fall out and be removed. I don't just air out my dirty laundry, I tend to wear it. His grace allows it. There's a tear in his eye regarding the pain, but I hear his godly giggle as he watches me run around in his love with no limits. Anything you ever need or want from me regarding my story and journey as it continues (and I still tend to screw it up), just let me know."

Here's what he wrote in his bio: "Most bios are written by the person themselves, but in the third person, as if someone is writing about them. I'm not going to do that. I'm just going to give you a brief glimpse of my journey, where it has led me to and therefore the purpose of this information." Chris then lists the areas where he had served and the fact that he did it with a high degree of success.

Then he continues:

"Underneath the surface, a silent storm was brewing. Underneath the surface . . . I was incredibly stressed out and exhausted from meeting everyone else's expectations. Rather than face my reality, I chose to cope with alcohol and hide. I was afraid to face my problem and horrified at the thought of anyone finding out. I had been a 'teetotaler' that preached boldly the absolute abstinence from and against the dangers of alcohol. Now I had become one [an alcoholic]. Image preservation gave way to reality when I found myself passed out, face down in my front yard, while my children watched through the window. The perfect preacher had fizzled out and had fallen, hard.

"There was nothing left, no image to maintain and I no longer cared what anyone thought. I entered a recovery ministry and encountered God in a way that

I had never known before. I found out that I hadn't fooled him. He knew all along about everything and yet, he loved me anyway. Along the journey I had to learn to forgive myself, to receive grace rather than frustrate it, to embrace the reality that no matter how far we fall or fail, there is hope. He can and does give beauty for ashes."

He then talks about the hard road he walked and how Jesus had walked it with him. Then he writes: "My concern, my passion, my burden now is for those who sit in our pews and fill our pulpits every week and appear all polished and perfect on the outside, but are coming apart on the inside. I want them to know that it's okay to come out of the dark, stick their head above ground, and share their struggles. My fear is that many of our churches are places for the perfect, rather than hospitals for the hurting. There are many more than we realize, sitting all around us as we wear our masks weekly and declare that we are 'fine.' My heart is to help those who are hurting, held back by their own personal hells, to help those who are affected by their friends or loved ones who struggle and just don't understand, and to help the church to understand that we are to be a place that is safe to admit our struggle and a place where healing can begin, and hope can be found."

I suspect many of you saying, "None of that is for me. I'm not that bad." Then there are others of you saying, "None of that is for me. I'm far worse than any example Steve could ever use."

If you don't think it's for you, I can't believe that you've read this far in this book without being offended and burning it. Actually, before you leave, let me say, "It's you! I don't care what your reputation is. It's you." Now you can go. If you ever have an attack of sanity, you can pick up this book again or give me a call. I've got some stuff that will help. If, on the other hand, you don't think this is for you because you're far worse than anything I've written, let me say, "It's you! I don't care how bad you are. It's you."

There is an old story about an elderly woman who came forward to take communion at her Anglican church. As she knelt at the communion rail, she started thinking about her sins. She was old and there had been a lot of sin. As the woman pondered who she really was, and looked up and down the communion rail at the others who were so clean and together, she tried, as the organ music played, to slowly, unobtrusively back away from the chancel. At that point the priest noticed her. He turned and stuck the communion cup of wine under her nose and said rather loudly, "Take it, woman! It's for sinners! It's for you." Remember the taste of the wine.

I love the parable of the prodigal son in Luke 15. The boy who ran away with his father's inheritance and blew it all on wine, women, and song had an attack of sanity and came home expecting more shame. Instead, he got a party. It's a wonderful story. If I had been at the party, during a band break, perhaps I would be outside smoking my pipe when the returned prodigal came out for a breath of fresh air. We would talk about his father's amazing love, the wonderful party, and the way he had been forgiven. Then I would tell him, if he would listen, "Son, tomorrow you have to go back to the fields, with the hot sun and harsh labor, but whatever you do and wherever you go, remember tonight, and don't ever forget the taste of the wine and the sound of the music."

What if we all, as it were, drank that wine? What if we remembered the taste of the wine and the sound of the music every time we worshiped or partied with other Christians, went to a Bible study, or had dinner and went to a movie with a Christian friend? What if the taste of the wine lingered every time we sang a song or hugged someone who also knew the taste of the wine? What if we remembered the taste of the wine and the sound of the music in every encounter with other Christians? What if, when we looked at their sin, experienced their shame, and tasted the salt of their tears, we remembered the taste of the wine and the sound of the music? What if the most obvious thing about a funeral, dinner, meeting, small group, counseling session, planning session, choir or band practice, church conference, or ministry effort was the memory of the taste of the wine?

In the next chapter I want to show you what it would look like to go to the world and hang out with other sinners who have not tasted the wine—the hungry, oppressed, lost, fearful, lonely, LGBT folks, homeless, conservatives like me, liberals like my friends, guilty, adulterers, liars, prominent, greedy, nobodies, rich, poor, Pharisees, prostitutes, clean, dirty, educated, and those who ran away from kindergarten. The results would be astounding, as long as we didn't forget the sound of the music and the taste of the wine.

But for now let's talk about family, family secrets, and family matters. Let's talk about church.

Rachel Held Evans's wonderful book *Searching for Sunday: Loving, Leaving, and Finding the Church* is organized around seven sacraments. In the book she takes her readers through the liturgical year to show that the church from which she ran—the church of hypocrites, politics, scandals, and scoundrels—is nevertheless God's church and Rachel couldn't get away from it. She talks about how the church advances, not through power and might, but through acts of "love, joy, and peace and missions of mercy, kindness, humility."

She writes, "In this sense, church gives us the chance to riff on Jesus' description of the kingdom, to add a few new metaphors of our own. . . . And even still, the kingdom remains a mystery just beyond our grasp. It is here, and not yet, present and still to come. Consummation, whatever that means, awaits us. Until then, all we have are metaphors. All we have are *almosts* and *not quites* and wayside shrines. All we have are imperfect people in an imperfect world doing their best to produce outward signs of inward grace and stumbling all along the way."[2]

It is incredibly important that we be as honest as possible about the reality of the church. That honesty is the key to everything else. I love the church but the love isn't a blind love that ignores the flaws. In reality, love enables the one who loves to see those flaws more clearly and to love despite them. I see them in me, in you, and in the institution. When Augustine suggested that the church was a prostitute but his mother, he had seen that reality. It's the reality that the church is often like a department store that advertises certain products in the store window but doesn't keep them in stock. We advertise release from guilt, but we're probably the most guilty people on the face of the earth. We advertise freedom, but it's astounding how often our religion has made us the opposite. Not only are we probably the most guilty people in the world, we're probably the least free. We advertise love but sometimes we're so unloving to one another, so judgmental, and so critical, that it's hard to find the love. Often, what you think you see isn't what you get.

Do you remember when Peter wore a mask (Galatians 2:11–14)? No, not when he denied Christ, but when he modeled godly leadership. It was a church meeting, and Peter was walking with Paul and affirming Paul's ministry. Everything was fine until some religious leaders showed up and Peter changed sides because he wanted to curry the favor of the people with power. We've all stumbled like that. But that Peter . . . led the church, stood for Christ, and ended up dying a martyr.

I have a psychologist friend, Tom Saunders, who wrote a book, *Go Ahead—Kill Yourself! Save Your Family the Trouble.*[3] It's a great book on a new and exciting kind of family therapy, but it is also a critique of the therapeutic/ counseling community. Among other things, Tom writes that most therapy is done by therapists with their own issues, and who are working out their stuff by counseling others and making a fairly good living at it. I told Tom, "If you ever wonder why you'll never get invited to lunch by your colleagues in this town (Orlando), it's because of that book. Are you crazy?"

What I'm writing here about the church is not dissimilar to what Tom wrote about therapy. We are both, in different venues, saying, "The emperor is buck naked." I wear a mask and have my hidden agendas and you do too. Hardly any brother or sister in Christ is what you think they are, and what you see isn't often what you get.

When I was a young pastor, I talked about a "call" (and I really do think I had a call, even if it was different from what I thought). But there was a lot more than that. I was dealing with significant guilt (some of it real and some of it not) and my agenda was to become really spiritual (that would be someone who is ordained, with only missionaries being more spiritual). Then I figured God would notice, forgive me, and maybe even like me and be proud of me. Of course, it didn't work, but I tried and sometimes still try.

Ronald Rolheiser has said that the church is made up of "scoundrels, warmongers, fakes, child molesters, murderers, adulterers and hypocrites of every description . . . and saints" and that "the church always looks exactly as it looked at the original crucifixion, God hung among thieves."[4]

Okay, point made. We're a bad, sinful, and needy lot. Deal with it!

Well, that's kind of abrupt.

Let me show you in the next chapter some ways to deal with it. I'm going to do that even if it doesn't matter.

Well, it does matter . . . but in a way that might surprise you.

Behind the Mask

1. In your own words, what is shame?
2. How are shame and fear connected?
3. What does the church really look like? What should it look like?
4. For those in relationship with you, how is "what you think you see isn't what you get" true in your life?
5. How do you identify with the prodigal son story?

Background Scriptures: Psalm 90:8; Isaiah 45:17; Isaiah 49:23; Joel 2:27–28; Romans 9:33; Romans 10:11; Romans 8:21; Luke 15

Note to small group leaders: Refer to these Scriptures as needed during your discussion, along with Scripture passages in the chapter.

CHAPTER 12

A New Kind of Family

If we walk in the light, as he is in the light, we have fellowship with one another . . . (1 John 1:7)

There is a great (and old) book by William Hendricks, *Exit Interviews*, reflecting his research on why people leave the church. A lot of church growth researchers stand at the front door of the church, as it were, and ask why people have come. They help create "seeker-driven" churches. Instead, Hendricks stood at the back door and asked people why they were leaving. It's a very insightful book in which Hendricks draws some profound conclusions. One is that the church often preaches God's amazing grace, but doesn't live it. Then Hendricks writes, referring to the stories in the book and his own frustration, "So why permit it? Why even tolerate it, especially when Jesus and Paul, among others, reserved their harshest words for those who compromised grace?"[1]

I share Hendricks's frustration. In fact I'm frustrated with myself sometimes. Everything I've written in this book is true and biblical. There will be a lot of people who will tell me (and maybe you) that I'm antinomian, that I encourage sin, and that I'm not faithful to the "whole counsel of God." While I often look at what I've written and see myself in the criticism, I don't see it there. Frankly, the critics don't know what they're talking about. They reflect the core of the problem of which you and I are a part.

Still, I'm seeing so many churches, so many books, and so many people I love grasp the importance of authenticity that it seems like a movement—and one for which I'm so glad. Yet the questions persist, as does the problem of "doing church" right. How do we create a church that is a "safe place"? Are there steps we can take to deal with our shame and the shame of our brothers and sisters? What can we do to make church (our family) better, more vulnerable, and yet safe? How can we do church in a way that permits us to laugh, sing, and dance? In short, what can we do?

The first answer to those questions is this: Nothing! There isn't a thing we can do. The problem is so systemic and difficult that nobody can "do" anything. If anything is done, it will have to be done by Jesus. Our fixes are so self-righteous (self-righteousness, of course, about the self-righteous), so angry, and so born out of frustration that our "fixes" will often make things worse. So many people who are reading this book will agree with what I've written—at least to a degree. Many people will think, *We must do something*, while others will make plans, think through the issues, preach sermons, write blogs and books (like this one) and "raise the flag." Some might even try to start a church where "we do it right and different."

In her book *Searching for Sunday*, Rachel Held Evans wrote about how she and some friends started a church that met in a funeral home. I asked her in an interview what happened to that church. "Well," she said, "it died." I said that I supposed that a church dying in a funeral home was appropriate. The answer isn't a new church, a new program, or a new discipleship curriculum. The answer is a new you and, if you can pull that off, you're a better man (or woman) than I am. That's the business of Jesus. It starts with a major realization that it's not (as the old spiritual puts it) "my brother, or my sister . . . it's me, O Lord, standing in the need of prayer."

How to Wear the Shoes of Grace

My friend Tom Sloan—a broadcaster, missionary, and pastor in Mexico—is an amazing man. He has a background that is quite traditional, very orthodox, and especially oriented in the direction of doing it right. He was doing fine with all of that until he hit a wall. Tom ended up leaving Mexico and very nearly left his faith. Then he discovered God's love—an unconditional love that, like the velveteen rabbit in Margery Williams's children's story, loved him into "realness." I talk to him often, and Tom is so radically loving and clear on God's grace that sometimes I talk to him just to remember what this thing is all about.

Tom is working on a book now, and in it he has a chapter called "Nebuchadnezzar and the Prodigal Son." I wish I could share the whole chapter with you, but Tom's main point is that both Nebuchadnezzar and the young son in Jesus's parable are prodigals with similar traits. Tom confesses that he's one too. (So am I, and so are you.) He writes:

> A prodigal is never a victim. Oh, he is foolish, reckless and a rebel, but not a victim. He may have been lied to about the nature of his father's love and grace, but in the end, the prodigal always makes his own decision to

go into the far country and he is fully responsible for that decision. . . . As a prodigal speaking to prodigals, I don't know if you can ever get over being a prodigal once you've been one. Those of us who have been prodigals have proven one thing—we could not live by the law. We could not be as good as they wanted us to be. We could not be as good as we wanted to be. . . . Could it be that we didn't know how much the Father loved us? Maybe we thought that the far country would be more of a thrill than the Father's love. . . . The prodigal's greatest fear is not being accepted, so he asks to be made as one of the Father's hired servants, working to prove his worth. Grace is almost too good to be true and this is why one of the most difficult things is accepting that we are accepted . . . even if the prodigal never does a good job working as a servant in the field. On the days I doubt that Abba Father has fully accepted me, all I have to do is look at the gifts he has given me—the ring on my hand and the shoes on my feet. The most amazing thing is that the shoes actually fit. Now, how did he know my exact shoe size?

So the most important thing is to wear the shoes, remember where you got them, and keep telling yourself that it's amazing they fit. Then do nothing but look at your new shoes and let Jesus love you. If you do no more than that, it will be sufficient. It will be sufficient because what Jesus has done is finished and sufficient. Nothing more has to be added. Nothing.

But you do have to walk around in your new shoes. While we're walking around, there are seven things I want you to remember. (I thought I would call it *The Seven Habits of Highly Effective People.* That title was already taken but it did sell a lot of books for Stephen Covey. Then I thought I could call it *The Seven Steps to Having a Shame-Free Ministry* or *The Seven Commandments of Living Grace.* That's when I thought the Holy Spirit said, "You've got to be kidding!" Or it could have been indigestion.) Finally, I decided that I would just give you some suggestions to remember.

1. Remember not to have expectations of yourself or others that are too high.

Someone told me once that I wouldn't be so shocked at my own sins if I didn't have such a high opinion of myself. Under this "place of remembrance" there is a sort of rule: Don't put (well, "Try not to put . . .") expectations on others that you shouldn't even have for yourself. Jesus told the prostitute in Luke 7 that she was loved. He didn't tell her that she should do better the next time or that she should watch it. He just said she was forgiven. Yeah, Jesus did tell the woman caught in adultery (John 8) that she should go and stop sinning, but that was a particular place with a particular circumstance, certainly not a way to put her on a trip of rules and regulations. Jesus had already pointed out to her that nobody (the guys with the rocks) could throw rocks at anybody because nobody was without sin. If she had gone back to her lover (who let her take all the fall by herself), Jesus would still have loved her because he wasn't a physician to well people but to sick ones. And that would be us.

The Christian faith isn't what we do for God; it's what he's done for us. Try to remember that. I've read so many books on how to get better, on making my life count, on standing for Jesus, and on being pure and good that I have grown weary. In fact, those times when I came the nearest to running away was when I tried hard and couldn't pull it off. Then I put on the mask they gave me when I was ordained and, as long as I could, I was able to play the role. When I finally couldn't do it anymore, I expected rejection. Instead Jesus said, "Finally!"

2. Remember that change comes slowly but change does come.

We teach a principle in Key Life's *Born Free* seminar: *You take the first small step and God will take the second one. By the time you reach the third step, you'll know that it was God who took the first small step.* Because the problem of shame, fear, and guilt is so great in us and in others, there is a tendency to just give up. Don't. When Longfellow said that the mills of God grind slowly but exceedingly fine, he was talking about justice and he was probably right. But he was absolutely right about the mills of God.

In Luke 17:20–21 Jesus made an amazing statement: "The kingdom of God is not coming in ways that can be observed, nor will they say, 'Look, here it is!' or 'There!' for behold, the kingdom of God is in the midst of you." In other words, you maybe can't see it, but even now (and your reading of this book may even be a part of it) God is doing his thing and he does it right well. That's his business and we've got to stop trying to do what is above our pay grade. But do trust the old guy (and the Bible) when I say that God is doing really good things in his church, in you, and in me.

For many years I've taught that God isn't angry with his people. Once during a conference's question-and-answer session, a man raised his hand and said, "I think you're wrong. God is angry with us and I'm glad he is. It keeps me doing the right thing." In my normal, kind, and gentle way,

I said to him, "Sir, you're a fruitcake. I get disagreeing with me, but being glad that God is angry is neurotic." He got angry and left the conference.

That's happened often over the years and, while I'm not sure I understand all the reasons, it is a phenomenon that goes with the "turf" of what I believe God has called me to do. In fact, there have been times when I thought I was the only one brave enough to teach radical grace without a kicker. (That thought, of course, was extremely narcissistic and insane, and the angels laughed at me. Nevertheless, there were times when I really did think, with some significant exceptions, I was the only one.) I wanted to be accepted and affirmed and, while there was some of that, there were the voices that said, "You have to be careful about Steve and this teaching because people will take advantage of it." Sometimes they said, "Steve is sincere but he never draws the line and we must, for God's sake and his holiness, draw the line." I was (and still am) called antinomian, irrelevant, and a teacher of a message of "easy believism" and "cheap grace."

I'm not whining about the critics here. They may be right, but they're probably wrong. It doesn't matter. Besides, I'm meaner than they are, have a thick skin, and frankly don't care much. Besides that, it lowers people's expectations of me, and I'm all for lowered expectations as they relate to me.

I often teach seminars at The Billy Graham Training Center (The Cove) in the mountains of North Carolina. Those seminars are advertised a year or so in advance and people who come to my seminars are either as weird as I am or have come to expect the radical nature of what I teach and are no longer surprised. But fairly recently, Cliff Barrows asked me to be the substitute teacher at a "Seniors Weekend" at The Cove. The advertised and well-known teacher had a major and unexpected conflict so, at the last minute, had to opt out. So Cliff asked me to come.

Most of the people there were major supporters of The Billy Graham Association; they were leaders in their local churches and communities; they were people who were known for their commitment to Christ and his people. They were, in short, people who were known for and defined by their Christian faith. Not only that, most of them didn't have the foggiest idea who I was. They knew I wrote books, was a broadcaster and a professor, but beyond that, they didn't know what to expect.

At the time, I was working on a fairly controversial book (*Three Free Sins*) and decided to use some of that material in my four sessions. I knew it would be fairly controversial to those folks but I figured that if they kicked me out, I would go out "in a blaze of glory." So I decided to clearly teach what I was learning . . . even if it got me in trouble.

To make a long story short, after the first session, those Christians were in shock. I think I heard a man near the front say to his wife, "I don't believe he's saved!" Others wouldn't look at me and, if it had been a church, nobody would have come out, taken my hand, and said, "Fine sermon, pastor."

But they came back for the second session and, to my surprise, some of them started to "get" it. More got the message in the third session and, by the last session, we all were very close to having a party celebrating God's grace and mercy to horrible sinners who finally understood that they didn't deserve to come to the party and were there by invitation. I was wearing a blue blazer in that last session and I was hugged so much and so often, that the blazer got terribly wrinkled and turned white with the face powder of some of the women who hugged me. As my wife and I were driving away from The Cove after the last session, my wife said, "Wow," and I said, "I don't think I've ever been affirmed so much in my entire life."

What happened? Those wonderful people were the "real deal." They really had worked hard at pleasing God, serving faithfully in their churches and Christian organizations. They wanted more than anything else to please the God who had called them. I told them that it wasn't enough and that was the bad news. Then I told them that God was already pleased and, instead of "doing more," they should just rejoice in the reality that was already theirs. Nobody had told them that or, at any rate, in that way. I said, "You don't fool me. I've been doing this too long and I've got your number. Every one of you has secrets that you've told no one and, if you told us your secrets, you would be so embarrassed that you would leave this conference in shame. You've worked so very hard but at night, when nobody is around, you know it's not enough . . . not nearly enough. You thought you would be a lot better by now, but you aren't. All of you wish you were as good, as committed, and as pure as people think you are . . . and you know you're not."

That, of course, was the bad news one has to hear before hearing the good news. I told them the good news too: Jesus knows all of that—all your secrets, all of your sins, and all of your failed efforts—and he is crazy about you. In fact, Jesus doesn't think he can have a party unless you're there. And not only that, there is nothing that will ever change what he thinks about you. It's forever. That's when the celebration began.

The reason I'm telling you all this is because, of late, I've been watching celebrations breaking out all over the country. I didn't expect it. I just figured I would keep doing what God told me to do until I drooled or died and wouldn't expect much. I thought that a few would get it but most wouldn't. In other words, over the years I had lowered my expectations to the point where I was thankful when I didn't lose too many. And then God (and it's so God) surprised me. I started getting letters, and calls, and emails. We got over a million "hits" on Key Life's website over the last twelve months. And it continues to grow.

I was a speaker at a conference recently that was filled to capacity—young and old, rich and poor, black and white, tattooed and necktied, sophisticated and pedestrian, bald and pigtailed, wing-tipped and sandaled, high-heeled and booted, dreadlocked and barbered—with people who had come to celebrate Christ's finished work on the cross. As I stood in the back of that auditorium, I realized that something had changed. In fact, the whole landscape had changed. I wept with joy at what God was doing. In fact, I believe that we are sitting on top of an awakening in America led by people who refuse to build walls, wear masks, foist agendas, or to pretend that they are anybody's mother.

I never thought it would happen, but it is and I wanted you to know.

3. Remember to wait and watch, and, whenever you can, speak truth to power . . . and to yourself.

We'll talk a lot more about this in the next chapter when we examine masks and mission, but let me say in passing that the main job of a Christian is to simply speak truth and not shilly-shally. One of the last things Jesus said to his disciples was this: "Go [in Greek, "as you're going"] into all the world and proclaim the gospel [i.e., the "good news"] to the whole creation" (Mark 16:15). I'm for that. But we need to do the same thing to one another, in our churches and at church meetings.

For the first time in my adult life, I'm part of a small group Bible study that I don't teach or lead. If one does what I do for a living, just showing up at a small group at church can skew the group dynamics. Because of the media thing, the books, and the seminary teaching, I am immediately the "guru" and everybody shuts up. (That, by the way, is insane. If they only knew . . .) However, both my wife and I felt led to become a part of a small group in our church. "Honey," my wife said lovingly but clearly, "this isn't going to work if you don't keep your mouth shut." I've done that except when I surprised people with my sin and with the fact that I didn't have the foggiest idea the answer to their questions. To be honest, I've done quite well, thank you. Not only that, I've experienced "real church" in a place I didn't expect it.

I've also become a cheerleader. The other night someone in our group went off on a rant about obedience, purity, and being faithful, and he gave a list. This member of the Bible study (not the teacher) gets grace, but, as with all of us, sometimes is frustrated with others and with himself. It wasn't that what this particular person said was wrong (he was right) but what he said put everybody in our small group into a "shame mode." It got very quiet. That was when a lady who never says anything spoke up and blushed as she did. "I feel bad," she said. "I don't do any of that. Don't get me wrong. I try, but I can't tell you how much I fail and in the areas you just mentioned." I was so excited about what she said that I almost spoke in tongues. (Presbyterians don't do that. It's unseemly.)

When the Bible study was over, I hugged that woman and whispered in her ear, "I'm so proud of you that I can hardly stand it! You go!" She left our group smiling. And I left feeling hopeful. It was, of course, a small venue, but she had spoken truth and it showed on all the faces in the room. You don't have to change the world, just the places where you can say something (speak truth) or do something (hug a dirty kid).

Jesus said that we should be "wise as serpents and innocent as doves" (Matthew 10:16). In chapter 2 I quoted my late mentor, when he said that the inappropriate and reckless ripping off of a mask was the kiss of death for friendship. He's right. In fact, let me suggest that you read that second chapter again and remember what I taught you. You have to be very careful to whom and in front of whom you take off your mask, as well as the timing of that removal. But that doesn't mean you shouldn't do it. If we're willing to reveal who we are in little pieces and to admit our hidden agendas in small places, it will become addictive. And it will become contagious.

I have a friend, a famous pastor (you would know his name) who was disgraced, with a great number of people bearing witness to the way they were shamed and demeaned by him. I've stayed in touch with him even though some friends have told me I shouldn't. At any rate, one friend told me that he was glad I was and then said, "What he really needs is someone to hug him." In order to do that, I have to be real to him about who I am. I hate that but I've been watching and waiting, and this just came along.

We've all heard a lot about "creating opportunities" to be witnesses for Christ. Forget that. You don't have to create opportunities. Just walk around in your new shoes and try to be sensitive to the opportunities God has given you to be real, to cut slack, and to set aside your hidden agendas. The people you touch will amaze you.

Just don't duck.

4. Remember that when you see God working on your shame— when the masks start coming off and the hidden agendas are no longer worth the effort—rejoice in it but don't talk too much about it.

In John 3:30, John the Baptist said that Jesus must increase and that he (John) must decrease. A friend of mine told me once about a frog who lived in the north and wanted to go south for the winter as the swans did. Each year that frog watched the swans fly south while he shivered in the snow and cold. Then he got an idea. He went to the swans and asked to go with them. "You can't fly!" they responded.

"I know," the frog said, "but I have a wonderful idea. Let me get a stick and if two of you will help me, I can go with you. Two of you could keep the ends of the stick in your beaks and I could hang on to the middle of the stick and get out of this miserable cold weather."

So two of his swan friends agreed to help and it worked beautifully for many miles. However as they were flying low over the farmlands of North Carolina, a farmer looked up and saw the frog holding onto the stick. "Look at that!" he shouted to a friend, "That's amazing! Wonder whose idea that was?"

The frog, quite proud of his incredible idea, opened his mouth to tell them. That's when he fell to his death.

Pride and self-righteousness are the most dangerous places for a Christian to live. C. S. Lewis said, "May God's grace give you the necessary humility. Try not to think— much less, speak—of their sins. One's own are a much more profitable theme! And if on consideration, one can find no faults on one's own side, then cry for mercy; for this must be a most dangerous delusion."[2]

One of the most joyous experiences of a Christian is the confession of sin to other Christians. (That's true, too, in confessing before unbelievers, and we'll talk about that in the next chapter.) One must be cautious, but once you've found a safe place, with safe people who are sinners and as bad as you are (and everybody is), the confession is an open door to freedom, forgiveness, and joy. However, one must be careful here. Confession is one thing. You would think it prevents self-righteousness, but it doesn't. A priest once cautioned a man confessing to him, "You're not confessing. You're bragging." He was giving him a serious warning. One can be quite proud of one's sins (a dark place to be) but even worse, one can also be quite proud of one's authenticity in making the confession.

A friend once said, "I have repented but have had to repent of my sinful repenting." I had no idea what he was talking about and asked him. "Steve, it's very easy to slip into the pride of asking Jesus to notice that I'm honestly confessing and repenting, while others aren't spiritual enough or honest enough to do what I'm doing." He's right. The frog can open his mouth and fall to his death.

That's neurotic, you're thinking. *You've created a "damned if you do and damned if you don't" scenario that's crazy.* Yes, it may be neurotic. There can be too much "navel-gazing" in Christians and, even if what I'm pointing to here is a good caution, there isn't a thing you can do to fix it. So don't obsess on it but do remember it.

5. Remember to give the family failure to Jesus and to party when you experience success.

When the church was just starting, before the persecution that was soon to follow, the book of Acts describes the family meetings: "And they devoted themselves to the apostles' teaching and fellowship, to the breaking of bread and the prayers. And awe came upon every soul, and many wonders and signs were being done through the apostles" (Acts 2:42–43). That sounds like a very "spiritual" gathering. I suppose it was, but it was more than that. It was a party.

I served as the pastor of one church for almost twenty years. The church had started years before in a bar. They had to clean up the beer cans on Sunday morning before they worshiped. As I look back at those years, I see a group of screwed-up and very sinful people learning about grace together. We didn't know it at the time. It's hard to see something that's profound when you're in the middle of it. I remember . . .

. . . The gay guy who stood up asking for help, and a bunch of people who surrounded him and loved him.

. . . The adulterous relationship between two couples. Each couple divorced so that they could marry the spouses of the other couple. They walked into the church—ashamed, guilty, and devastated by the results of their actions. To their surprise, they found other sinners who welcomed them, and didn't make excuses but rejoiced in their repentance (i.e., "attack of sanity").

. . . The man who had been a deacon in another church before divorcing his wife to marry the pastor's wife. I remember him telling me how a member of the previous church had chased him down with a gun and tried to kill him. I remember their coming to our church, so rejected and ashamed. I remember the clarity of their confession and how, on many occasions, I sent people to that couple for help with their own marriages. I had come to trust their honesty about the pain of their sin and their refusal to wear a mask or create a hidden agenda of self-justification.

. . . The woman who kept sleeping and snoring on the front row during worship. The ushers let her sleep because they figured "she needed the sleep more than the sermon."

. . . The drunk who came to a worship service so plastered that if we had struck a match the place would have blown up—and the people who surrounded him, loved him, and gave him coffee.

. . . The baby who was baptized while his mother stood by without a husband . . . and the other singles in the congregation standing in a circle around her and her baby, pledging that they would be "the father."

. . . The times the pastor (that would be me) said and did sinful and stupid things, and was loved anyway.

The . . . well, it goes on and on, and I must stop. I can't tell you how grateful I am for those memories.

At any rate, when my wife and I moved to central Florida so that I could teach in the seminary, one Christmas we searched out members of that church who also had moved here. There were a lot of them. We invited them over for a Christmas party . . . and we did party. We sat around sharing "war stories," laughing and crying. I'll never forget what one lady said: "We were part of a sort of Camelot and we didn't even know it."

That's what heaven will be like—sitting around the fire of God's presence telling war stories. It will be one of the best things about heaven. But, because God likes us, he lets us experience a bit of that before heaven. Don't miss those times. Anna, my wife, is recognized in our family as the "creator and identifier of memories." That's what all of us should be. You can't party while you're adjusting a mask and fostering any agenda other than the party.

So don't forget to party.

6. Try to remember that it won't last.

Well, it will, but not until we get Home. The trouble with a church that learns to be real is that there is also another crowd coming and another generation that "knew not Joseph." It's one of the reasons revivals and awakenings generally only last one generation. Also, if what I've described here is true (and it is) and there really is a Devil (and there is), his priority is to divert, divide, and confuse God's love. He wants to add "kickers" and to make those who are free turn religious and sour. It's the reason Martin Luther said that we must preach the gospel to each other lest we get discouraged.

That's it.

"Wait, wait," you say. "I thought you had seven things we should remember." I know. I lied about the seven. There are only six.

Okay. For the sake of honesty, let me give you one more.

7. Rejoice and be glad when people leave.

I know that doesn't sound very Christian, but it is. In the final chapter (the Q&A chapter), I'll talk about church discipline, which John Calvin said was one of the signs of the "true church." It's not what you think it is, but sometimes it does bring revival. Someone said that if you find a perfect church, don't join it. You'll screw it up. Good point that. Let me give you another one: When people get so angry, so uptight, and so concerned about the freedom and transparency of a particular church and leave, be a little sad and pray for them, but then get a bottle of champagne and celebrate, because God is getting ready to do something amazing.

My friend Chuck Holliday is a pastor who gets grace and has paid a big price to get it. His wife Debbie is incredibly honest. Both Chuck and Debbie were virgins when they got married and Debbie, in a moment of frustration over Chuck's self-righteousness, said to him, "Sometimes I think it would have been a lot better if, when we married, you had not been a virgin." Chuck eventually understood that he was a lot worse than he thought he was and that God's grace (as Jack Miller said) was a lot bigger than he thought it was. And not only that, he used what Debbie had said to him in a sermon, adding his comments, "We must understand the gospel. While virginity and sexual purity are good things, virginity and sexual purity are not the gospel." (I don't know if I would have said that but Chuck did, and it's one of the reasons I love him.)

At that moment a big man—the father of eight kids, and a very angry and intolerant father and husband—stood up and said quite loudly, "That's it! We're out of here!" He pointed to his kids and wife, and said, "Let's go." With that, the entire family (all ten of them) marched out of the church. Chuck said he didn't know what to say and that it was very quiet in the church.

If I had been there (and knowing Chuck, it might have been what he did say), I would have said, "Let's stop and pray for our brothers and sisters who just left. After we do that, let's adjourn this worship service and party!"

If you read this chapter, you know why.

Behind the Mask

1. Is it really possible to have expectations that are too high? Why or why not? What happens when they are too high?

2. When it comes to dealing with our shame, fear, and guilt, change is a long and slow process. How have you found this principle—You take the first small step and God will take the second one . . . By the time you reach the third step, you'll know that it was God who took the first small step—true in your life? How do you trust God in the process?

3. How can you "speak truth" to yourself and others? What is the result when you do?

4. Do you really believe that the Devil's priority is to "divert, divide, and confuse God's love . . . to add 'kickers' and to make those who are free turn religious and sour"? How successful has he been in your life and in the church? What are the signs of hope?

Background Scriptures: 1 John 1:7; Luke 7; John 8; Luke 17:20–21

Note to small group leaders: Refer to these Scriptures as needed during your discussion, along with Scripture passages in the chapter.

CHAPTER 13

Masks and Mission

For though I am free from all, I have made myself a servant to all, that I might win more of them. . . . I have become all things to all people, that by all means I might save some. Now this I do for the sake of the gospel, that I may share with them in its blessings. (1 Corinthians 9:19, 22–23)

I once heard a missionary speaker tell about a church meeting where everyone got into such a strong disagreement that it turned into a shouting match and then a brawl. It got so bad that the police had to be called. One of the police officers—a Buddhist—was heard to yell over the melee, "Why can't you people act like Christians?" Acting like Christians is the subject of this chapter and it's not what you think.

I was once the pastor of a church where we did no formal evangelism. I felt guilty about that because evangelical pastors are supposed to teach their people how to "share their faith." I believe evangelism training often helps people to feel they can do something they could have done quite well without the training; nevertheless, I still felt guilty. The problem was that every time I thought about organizing evangelism training classes, I would look around the church and see a lot of new Christians. I wondered why that was so; looking back, I have an answer. People were becoming Christians not because of apologetics (a formal defense of the Christian faith), smart people who were models (we weren't that smart), or good people who won others to Christ with their goodness (we weren't that good either). The reason evangelism worked without evangelism training is that we were using the most powerful evangelistic tool that Jesus ever gave his church. "Cold" people would notice our fire and come, as it were, to get warm.

I have a pastor friend, Sandy Wilson, who says that the problem in the church is that Christians are on the inside of the church with their noses glued to the window, watching the parties outside the church and wishing they could be there. Sandy says that he wanted a church where people outside the church had their noses glued to the windows, watching the parties inside and wishing they could come in.

Jesus prayed that Christians would be one "so that the world may believe that you [God] have sent me" (John 17:21). In John 13 Jesus told his disciples to love one another; then he said we should love one another so the world would know that we were his disciples. It's about us and not about them.

But it's about them too, because what happens in the church (and what I've written about in this book) is extremely important for "them." We really are here for "them"; that is the mission of the church. But before hungry people can be drawn to the smell of the food we offer, it has to be cooked in the church kitchen.

God has called his people into relationship with one another so that, among other things, we might experience how he has taught us to live. That means a central priority for the Christian who is serious about Jesus must be the removal of masks and the shredding of hidden agendas. If the church isn't a safe place for us, it won't be a safe place for anybody else. If we are marked by judgment of one another, shock at our own sins, and church discipline to keep the church "pure," we will build a wall that people will see, can't climb over, and from which they will walk away.

A friend gave me an anonymous piece that a lot of people have seen online or through social media. It's called "The Wall" and it is incredibly sad.

Their wedding pictures mocked them from the table, these two whose minds no longer touched each other. They lived with such a heavy barricade between them that neither a battering ram of words nor artilleries of touch could break it down. Somewhere, between the oldest child's first tooth and the youngest daughter's graduation, they lost each other.

Throughout the years, each slowly unraveled that tangled ball of string called self, and as they tugged at stubborn knots, each hid his searching from the other. Sometimes she cried at night and begged the whispering darkness to tell her who she was. He lay beside her, snoring like a hibernating bear, unaware of her winter. She took a course in modern art, trying to find herself in colors splashed upon a canvas, and complaining to other women about men who were insensitive. He climbed into a tomb called "the office," wrapped his mind in a shroud of paper figures, and buried himself in customers.

Slowly, the wall between them rose, cemented by the mortar of indifference. One day, reaching out to touch each other, they found a barrier they could not penetrate, and recoiling from the coldness of the stone, each retreated from the stranger on the other side. For when love dies, it is not in a moment of angry battle, nor when fiery bodies lose their heat. It lies panting, exhausted, expiring at the bottom of a wall it could not scale.

That happens in marriages, but it also happens with the family of God.

In the beginning there is joy . . . one is forgiven and knows that forgiveness is so necessary. There is meaning and it brushes away all agendas except the agenda of Jesus, and there is great freedom. But things happen, and slowly that love for God grows cold. We should have a new Sunday school class in the church: "The Angry, Troubled, Offended, and Shocked Sunday School Class." If you join that class (and I visit it sometimes), first things become secondary and we start majoring in the minors. The world to which we have been sent becomes less and less important and the "leaven" sits in a lump, turning rancid, moldy, and useless. Love dies and, with its death, the masks become impenetrable and the hidden agendas bolder.

Christian psychologist and author Dan Allender, speaking at a pastor's meeting sponsored by Key Life, said that biblical grace was so unbelievable, so amazing, so counterintuitive that most people in the church couldn't deal with it all at once. What's more, if pastors weren't careful, they could lose their jobs teaching it. "So," he said, "you have to teach it in small doses until you get your kids through college." Then Allender said that it must be taught, because if the pastor doesn't teach it, the pastor will create a place so hard that the pastor can't live there himself. "So," he suggested, "grace must be taught, not only for the sake of your people but for you."

That's true. Masks kill us and the love we once had, the first love we knew we desperately needed. The ecclesiastical agendas of power, self-righteousness, and protection are a part of our fallen human DNA, and gradually we go "the way of all flesh." Then we die. That, of course, is profoundly sad, but, in fact, Jesus will still love us. We're still forgiven and acceptable. But the tragedy is that the world will be bereft of our laughter and love. And, after all, we are here for them too. The love must not die in us and in our midst because when it does, it will die for them as well.

So let's talk about them.

They're Wrong and We're Right

I know, I know, that's a bit absolute. We are often wrong about politics, music, society, and a lot of other particulars. But with that being said, we're right about Jesus. And because we're right about Jesus, we're generally right about "first things" like meaning, eternity, right and wrong, good and evil, and God's revelation of himself.

That's good, but there is a sense in which it is also very dangerous. It's dangerous for everybody, but for Christians it is big-time dangerous because being right can be a doorway to self-righteousness, pride, arrogance, triumphalism, and elitism, the very things that destroy the power of the Christian faith in the world. Being right is the stuff of masks because when one is right about one thing, it's a short step to proclaiming not only one's truth but also one's wisdom, goodness, and purity. That's a mask. It's just one more step from there to creating all kinds of agendas to protect the

189

territory of our wisdom, goodness, purity, and the perks that go with it.

What starts out as an affirmation of truth, and thankfulness that God told us the truth, ends up being a lie that destroys the very truth we proclaim.

We've got a conundrum that Satan uses, maybe as much as anything in his arsenal, to destroy the mission of the church. We're right about truth and being right has often made us mean, judgmental, and arrogant. There are three things that have to be said about the truth that is so precious to us. If we can remember them, we'll be okay. (1) First, the truth isn't our truth. It was given to us as a gift and thus we are beggars, as someone said, telling other beggars where we found bread. (2) Second, while we have truth, we don't come anywhere close to living by that truth; thus we are beggars telling other beggars where we found bread. (3) Third, we often get the truth we've been given wrong, thus we are beggars telling other beggars where we found bread. The problem is hardly ever the truth. The problem is in us, those who speak truth.

Do you remember what happened to Dan Cathy, the president of Chick-fil-A, when he expressed his personal Christian convictions about marriage (he thinks it is a union between a man and a woman) and sex (be believes in a biblical sexual standard)? Almost immediately there was an organized, highly publicized, and furious boycott of Chick-fil-A. The anger and hatred expressed in that boycott was intense. Then there was another, highly publicized "Chick-fil-A Appreciation Day," where millions of people across the country bought millions of the food chain's products to protest those who had protested. I did too. Frankly, I'm probably the only person in the universe who doesn't like Chick-fil-A, but on that day I went to our local Chick-fil-A store and bought more chicken than I could eat. I was feeling pretty good about my stand. *I guess we showed them,* I thought.

Then I read Scott Sauls's book *Jesus Outside the Lines,*[1] where Scott tells "the rest of the story." Dan Cathy did not participate in or even encourage "Chick-fil-A Appreciation Day." (I thought he did.) Not only that, Cathy sought out his strongest critic, Shane Windmeyer, a major gay activist who abhorred everything Cathy stood for, and determined to be his friend. (That was a surprise.) Cathy listened to and affirmed Windmeyer's concerns, and built trust by caring, listening, and showing understanding. (That's a good thing, I suppose.) They became friends. (Wow.) And not only that, Windmeyer has "come out of the closet" and admitted to being Dan Cathy's friend, even writing positive things about him. (How about that?) The most important and amazing thing about that whole story is that Cathy not once changed his views or set aside what he believed was the truth about marriage and sex.

That's when I tried to take back the food I bought at Chick-fil-A on "Appreciation Day." They wouldn't take it back. So I went to God and told him that I had been wrong and thanked him for having a Christian brother like Dan Cathy, who knows that Jesus is more important than sex, sin, politics, or money. I repented "in dust and ashes." I also learned a truth that I've now shared with you. It's not the truth, dummy (that would be me, and you sometimes). It's the one who speaks the truth.

If you're a Christian, you can't compromise the truth. It's countercultural truth and just because it is true, it will sometimes offend, disturb, and repulse those who hear it. If we change, alter, or spin what God has said, we not only leave a smudge on the Bible page, we don't have anything to offer to anyone. You see, it's that very truth that grants freedom, joy, and meaning—food to hungry people—while at the same time causing others to run in a different direction, elbows and heels flying in the wind. Do remember, however, that aside from the truth propositions (theological/doctrinal) that are so important, Jesus said that he was the truth (John 14:6) and that when he was lifted up (on the cross and before the world) he would draw "all people" to himself (John 12:32).

For some reason God has chosen imperfect, sinful, and needy people (that would be us) through whom Jesus, the Truth, will speak and love. It's what Paul meant when he said that he was "crucified with Christ" and that Christ was living his life through Paul (Galatians 2:20). If what I just wrote is true (and it is), let me give you some suggestions that might help in dealing with your brothers and sisters in Christ and in the mission of God's people to the world.

You can't do any of this while wearing a mask and having an agenda other than truth, but if you're willing to risk, I promise God will show you things that will cause you to stand up and sing the "Hallelujah Chorus."

There are those both inside and outside the family of God who think they have us figured . . . so shock them.

I'm often taken with the great variety among God's people found in the Bible. There are scoundrels and saints, intellectuals and kindergarten dropouts, rich and poor, rebels and those who dislike rebels, handsome and homely, sophisticated and pedestrian, leaders and followers, the weird ones and the normal, and radical types and establishment types. And we all belong to one another. When Paul was talking about the different gifts given to Christians, what he said is relevant to the problem of "sameness." "Now there are varieties of gifts, but the same Spirit; and there are varieties of service, but the same Lord; and there are varieties of activities, but it is the same God who empowers them all in everyone" (1 Corinthians 12:4–6). Then he said that the Christians with certain and different gifts should never say to people with other gifts, "I have no need of you" (1 Corinthians 12:21).

That is specifically about spiritual gifts, but the principle works for all of us. Even if some people in our family would like for us to be the same, to like the same music, to go to the same movies, to hold the same political views, to worship the same way, to eat the same Christian cookies, and wear the same Christian underwear, it's never going to happen. And God designed it that way. So offending and shocking other Christians is sometimes in order.

But it's in order for those who are not in our family too. Unbelievers think they know what we're going to say (so, for God's sake, say something different), what we enjoy (so, for God's sake, don't hide what you enjoy), and what we think (so, for God's sake, think some things that are out of the Christian box). Do that for God's sake . . . but also for their sakes. In other words, we do no service to the cause of Christ when we appear to be something less than normal human beings doing the normal human things that normal human beings do. Of course, we're called to be "in the world" and not "of the world" (John 17:14–16), but Jesus isn't talking about our goodness, our sameness, and our Christian weirdness. He's talking about our love for him and for those to whom he sends us. So take off your mask, and go and shock somebody. If you have to do it, offend them.

193

There are those both inside and outside the family of God who think we are good, pure, and nice people (or, at minimum, think that we think we are good, pure, and nice people) . . . so disabuse them.

When we joined the church, or were baptized, or even participate in worship, we are making a statement about who we are. What we are isn't very pretty. We make a public proclamation that we're in great need, horrible sinners without hope except in Christ, and we don't know where else to go.

I love to sing the old hymn out of India, "I have decided to follow Jesus, no turning back, no turning back. The world behind me, the cross before me. No turning back, no turning back." That expresses the desire of my heart and the passion of my life. But can we talk?

Sometimes the world is before me and the cross is behind me, and there are those periods when I do turn back and become enamored with the harsh bark of the con men. Sometimes I really do screw it up. That's not a brief for sin; it's just a fact. I'm better except when I'm worse. I'm sanctified except when I'm not. I'm faithful except when I'm unfaithful. And the truth is that I not only described who I am, I described who you are.

So go and tell your Christian brothers and sisters. They will say, "I don't believe I would have said that." Then go tell people who aren't a part of your Christian family. They will also say, "I don't believe I would have said that." But both those outside and inside will think (and sometimes say in a whisper), "You too?" Then send them to Jesus.

There are those both inside and outside the family of God who think we are hypocrites . . . so "second that motion."

Let me show you something you may not have considered. If hypocrisy can be defined as someone who proclaims one thing and does the opposite, hypocrisy is not a proper charge to direct at Christians. If the Bible tells us that sin is universal, and that Christians don't live as outsiders to the human race, Christians are not hypocrites when they affirm that reality. They may be greedy, dishonest, unloving, lacking in compassion, rebellious, and horribly sinful, but, as bad as that is, Christians who don't live up to the standards of Scripture are *not* hypocrites.

That being said, it *is* true that the Bible gives a standard and Christians often don't live up to it. So if that is the definition of hypocrisy, then the proper answer to people who aren't a part of the church "because the church is full of hypocrites" should be clear: "Bingo! And that goes for me too!"

I told you earlier about Scott Sauls's book *Jesus Outside the Lines*. We interviewed Scott on our talk show and he said, "Of course I'm a hypocrite. That goes without saying. The question is, 'What kind of hypocrite am I?'" Scott wrote, "As strange as it may sound, it is the hypocrisy of Christians in the Bible that sometimes encourages me more than anything else. It reminds me that God's relentless grip on me, not my relentless grip on God, keeps me in his love. It reminds me that if there is hope for prostitutes and crooks and adulterers and racists and elitists and murderers and terrible husbands and coveters, there is hope for somebody like me."[2]

Again, I'm not giving you a brief for sin. You already know how destructive sin is and how clear the Bible is about it. The thing to remember is that we really *are* hypocrites and we don't have anything to defend—certainly not ourselves or the church. Now take off your mask and tell somebody, then laugh and tell them about Jesus.

There are those both inside and outside the family of God who think we are greedy . . . so give stuff away.

In Luke 9:3, when Jesus sent his disciples out to proclaim the kingdom of God, he said, "Take nothing for your journey, no staff, nor bag, nor bread, nor money; and do not have two tunics." Then in Luke 22:36 he says, "But now let the one who has a moneybag take it, and likewise a knapsack. And let the one who has no sword sell his cloak and buy one." Now, without going into the reasons Jesus said the exact opposite thing on these two occasions, let me say that, at minimum, he is saying that "stuff" is of no import except insofar as it is useful in the lives and work to which he has called us.

Christians aren't usually called to live lives of poverty, but they are called to recognize what is important and what isn't. Only a fool clings to those things that will be ultimately taken away. The trouble with people who eat right, live right, and exercise right is that on their deathbeds they will die of nothing; they will be like a sinking ship with nothing to throw overboard. But they will die and the question is . . . who will all the stuff belong to (Luke 12:20)? In other words, stuff isn't worth a bucket of spit.

(Well, that's a bit strong. My wife and I once went through a very large hurricane and lost our house and much of our stuff. I found out that stuff was more important to me than I thought it was, but I also found out that stuff was less important than I thought too.)

Here's the thing to remember. The stuff we own becomes a part of the mask we wear, and protecting our stuff often becomes our hidden agenda. A nice car isn't just a car, an expensive cigar isn't just a cigar, and stuff isn't just stuff. It can start to define us. That's the mask and the reason for the agenda. Christians who walk with Christ increasingly understand that; it is one of the reasons that the closer we get to him, the less important the mask is. There's something about love that creates love; there's something about having received compassion that creates compassion; there's something about being unconditionally accepted that fosters acceptance of others; and there's something about being helped that creates help for others.

I almost always give a dollar to the homeless who "will work for food" when they ask. I know they are probably going to use what I give them for drugs or booze. But Jesus did say that if they asked, I should give. Besides, it helps with my guilt. My friend, Buddy Greene (the Nashville singer) will generally give ten dollars. But when you give ten instead of one, you have to talk to them. So, as it were, give the ten. Look for places to have an open hand and then, to mix the metaphor, get some dirt under your fingernails. Touch the hungry and the outcasts (here and around the world) with your hands and with your words. One can only do that insofar as one is willing to take off the mask. It will confuse them and you'll smell like Jesus.

There are those both inside and outside the family of God who wonder who made us the boss of them . . . so don't be anybody's mother.

In Luke 12:14, Jesus said to the man who wanted Jesus to "fix" his brother, "Man, who made me a judge or arbitrator over you?" Paul wrote to the Romans, "Who are you to pass judgment on the servant of another? It is before his own master that he stands or falls" (Romans 14:4). In other words, we aren't called to be anybody's mother and we do way too much of that—or at least I do. One of the refreshing things about taking off one's mask is that you become less critical of those who wear theirs.

I'm very traditional and biblical in my views on sexuality, marriage, and morality. A number of years ago I got a letter very critical of those views. The writer was gay and he was angry. He wrote, "How dare you say that I'm not Christian and don't love God as much as you do!" Sometimes I ignore that sort of thing, but that day I was closer to Jesus than I am sometimes.

"I didn't say that! You didn't listen," I wrote back. "In fact, I would never say that. Given that I'm worse than you are, more needy than you are, and have screwed it up far more than you have, I would be crazy to say that. All I said was that I get hugged by God more than you do, not because I'm better, but because I'm worse. You don't get hugged much because you don't think you need a hug. Besides that, I'm not your judge or your mother."

Do you know what happened? We became friends.

Gigi Graham (one of the most authentic and transparent Christians I know) told me one time that she had given up judging anybody in the church or outside the church. Instead she said that she had decided just to do her best to love them. Then she said, "I asked my father about it. And he said I was right." She was.

If I can't fix myself, I certainly can't fix you. So I give up.

You have to give up your mask before you give up the "mother role." When you do, you'll be amazed at what happens and the wonderful freedom you'll experience.

There are those both inside and outside the family of God who think the church is irrelevant and weak . . . so agree with them and let Jesus do some of the work.

I'm a Presbyterian and we say we believe that God is absolutely sovereign. (I, of course, wouldn't suggest that you have to be a Presbyterian to be saved, but why take a chance?) The truth is that we really don't believe it. Nobody works harder at helping God out than Presbyterians. Paul writes, "For from him [God] and through him and to him are all things" (Romans 11:36). What would happen if we really believed that? What would happen if we decided that having political and religious leverage, social acceptance, and power was way above our pay grade? What if we let God be God without our help and instead got a milkshake? We don't have to please him to get accepted anymore (he's already pleased); we don't have to be good to curry his favor (he already likes us); and we don't have to pretend when we can't pull it off (he knew all about us before he loved us without condition).

Everything we have, everything we are, and everything we believe are from him. It's a gift we didn't earn. All we have to do is rip off the mask and shred the agenda, look around, find out where Jesus is doing his work, and run to catch up so we can watch . . . and then enjoy the celebration of what he has done.

Finally there are those both inside and outside the family of God who think there are places where Christians won't go and people Christians won't befriend . . . so go everywhere and hug everybody.

I had an uncle (a Methodist) who used to say that Baptists were like weeds. "They are everywhere," he would say, laughing, "and you can't get rid of them." That's what Christians are supposed to be—weeds. There are certainly enough of us.

So, I commission you in the name of Christ to get rid of the mask. You don't need it anymore. Then go everywhere and hug everybody "in Jerusalem and in all Judea and Samaria, and to the end of the earth" (Acts 1:8).

Behind the Mask

1. What is our mission as Christians? How do masks and hidden agendas stand in the way of that?
2. How is being right dangerous?
3. In what ways can you shock, disabuse, and unconditionally love people (both those inside and outside of God's family)? What happens when you do? Give examples.
4. In what way is the charge of our hypocrisy a true and valid one?
5. How is the stuff you own a part of the mask you wear, and protecting that stuff your hidden agenda?
6. Are you tempted to try to fix others (becoming their "mother")? How is that an impossible task to which you aren't even called?

7. What would really happen if we "decided that having political and religious leverage, social acceptance, and power was way above our pay grade? What if we let God be God without our help and instead got a milkshake?"?

Background Scriptures: 1 Corinthians 9:19, 22–23; John 17:20–21; John 13:34–35; 1 Corinthians 12:4–21; Luke 12:14; Romans 14:4; Romans 11:36

Note to small group leaders: Refer to these Scriptures as needed during your discussion, along with Scripture passages in the chapter.

CHAPTER 14

I'm Glad You Asked

For we know in part . . . but when the perfect comes, the partial will pass away. (1 Corinthians 13:9–10)

If you haven't noticed, I generally write in an exceedingly colloquial style (it drives editors nuts), teach a number of things without qualifiers (I just grow tired of "kickers"), and say things that I probably shouldn't say (disturbing my staff, my wife, and my mother were she still alive). So in some of the books I've written, I include a chapter dealing with some (but not all) of the questions that come up. Part of that is self-protection and part of that is clarification. Sometimes that helps and other times not so much.

But I still keep trying. Let me try again.

What about sin? You sometimes appear not to care about what the Bible says about right and wrong. Do you care?

Of course I care. I care a lot.

Have you ever seen those GEICO commercials where someone asks another person if they know that GEICO could save them 15 percent on their car insurance? That person replies in a rather snarky way, "Everybody knows that." Then the person who asks the question says, "But did you know that trees falling in a forest when nobody hears do make a noise, that words can really hurt you, that bad news doesn't always travel fast, that playing cards with Kenny Rogers gets old pretty fast, etc., etc.?" I love those commercials and they always crack me up.

Is God clear about sin? Is sin destructive? Should people stop sinning? Should I stop sinning? Of course! Everybody knows that, but did you know about forgiveness, love, and how God really changes people? There are many who spend a lot of time on sin and obedience, and I get that. Frankly, it would be less controversial if I did. The problem is that I've noticed that most people already know about their sin and they already feel guilty about it. I know I do. Almost everybody I know wants to be better than they are, so I decided not to beat it to death.

Speaking of getting better, you sometimes seem to be saying that we'll never get better. What about sanctification? What about "growing in grace"?

Oh, I believe deeply in sanctification. It's how I became a spiritual giant. I just don't want to brag about it because I don't want to be like the man who won his club's medal for being the most humble man of the year. They took it away when he started wearing it.

And if you believe that, you'll believe anything. But I really am better.

A week after I suffered a fairly mild coronary (if any coronary can be called "mild"), I was speaking at an event where Buddy Greene was the singer. He said (he doesn't have any respect for the clergy and thought it was funny), "You have to be careful about Steve and this heart attack thing. He'll take advantage of it and work it to death." He was right. I got more illustrations out of that than anything that has happened to me in the last ten years. I would go through a lot for a good illustration.

When Buddy joked about my heart attack, he made a point about most everything we do and especially about our faithfulness, our obedience, and our growth. On another occasion Buddy was talking about some things he had trouble achieving. He told me that he had asked God about it and God said, "Buddy, if I give you an inch, you'll take a mile." We all do that. It's a part of our nature. The truth is that our obedience is irrelevant to everything important. As I mentioned before, Martin Luther once said that neither us nor God needed our good works, but our neighbors did. He was right.

Okay. How do we get better?

We are constrained, motivated, and changed by the love of God (2 Corinthians 5:14). In Romans 2:4, Paul says that God is kind and his kindness is meant to lead us to the throne and to repentance. If we get better by "spit and elbow grease," it won't last. I've tried. I mean, I've really tried hard. I gave it up because it wasn't working. If you let Jesus love you and go on about your business, you'll get better. You'll still have a long way to go, but I promise that you'll get better, because "getting better" is no longer the issue. And then, because God likes us and wants to encourage us, on occasion he'll let us see what he's doing in our lives—the love we didn't have before, the obedience that is growing, the faithfulness that is slowly taking place. He doesn't do that very often because he knows we'll take advantage of it.

You mentioned "repentance." What is that?

I've written about repentance in a lot of places because we so often get it wrong. The word "repentance" is from a Greek word meaning "to change one's mind." Repentance isn't changing. I think we've already established that that's hard and doesn't happen as often as we think it does. But our attitude (which is what repentance really is) is changed by walking with Christ, being properly horrified by how often we fail, and being convicted by the Holy Spirit. Repentance isn't changing; it's God's methodology of changing us if he is of a mind to do so. Here's a working definition of repentance, always done in the context of Scripture in general and God's law in particular: Repentance is knowing who you are, who God is, and what you've done, and going to him with it. That kind of repentance is the source of unbelievable spiritual power. And not only that, Christians aren't just to repent; we are called to live lives of repentance.

While I was writing the answer to this very question, a close friend of mine who has HIV (I dedicated a previous book to him) sent me an email. He was talking about repentance and this is what he wrote: "I repented this morning. I've asked *forgiveness* for my sins 70 x 7 times, but this morning, I told God I didn't know better than him. In times past, I've let my emotions lead me astray and into sin. I thought I knew better than God in what I needed to satisfy my heart, to ease my pain, and to heal my wounds. This morning, I repented of my arrogance and for my lack of faith. I simply bowed and told him he knows better than I—in everything."

That's it.

Isn't it dangerous to reveal too much of ourselves? We live in a culture where there are no secrets left untold and no sin left unconfessed. That seems quite narcissistic.

I agree. It can be very dangerous. God doesn't call you, as it were, to take your clothes off in public. You be careful out there. And if that doesn't answer your question, go back and read chapter 2. If that still doesn't answer your question, ask me again and I'll try to clarify.

What about church discipline?

I wish I had a better word than "discipline." Go and read Hebrews 12, where the writer describes the wise and gentle hand of a loving Father. That means that God's discipline is usually short-lived and we know exactly what's happening when it's happening. It should be the same way in the church.

Church discipline should never be for sin. If it were, nobody would be left but you and me, and I'm quite concerned about you. Discipline is not for sin but for a lack of repentance (see above). A better way to put it is that discipline should be administered for wearing too many masks and not admitting it, and for hidden agendas that foster the lie of the mask.

What about truth?

It's all about truth. It's all about God's truth. Jesus said that he was "the truth" and that means that wherever truth is spoken, from profound theological insights, to politics, to history, to the multiplication tables, Jesus is present. As I said earlier in this book, we must never compromise any truth, but we must be very careful when and how we speak it. It's not so much about truth but the one who speaks truth. Jesus is the primary speaker of truth. Look at how he did it and "follow in his footsteps."

Will everybody like us?

Are you crazy? What I've written in this book will be like a "stick in a hornet's nest" to a whole lot of people. If you are into being liked (and aren't we all?) burn this book. Some will "rise up and call us blessed." We'll join hands and walk together. Others will throw rocks. But we will be dangerous and people won't laugh. It's time we stopped pretending and speak clear truth about us and about the world.

There is a danger in "getting" how radical grace is. The danger is that we can become all warm and fuzzy and forget about the truth. People who don't have anything to protect really are dangerous. They can speak truth (even hard truth) to the world without compromise and without trying to spin it. When we do that, the love we have been loved with does make us kinder, gentler, and more compassionate. It also keeps us under the reality that we are the "chief" of sinners. Sometimes that will cause people to like us, but not always. We interviewed N. T. Wright on our talk show last week. He talks a lot about the kingdom and even more about the King. We are now part of a kingdom with a King nobody elected and nobody will depose. He is a King who knows us and loves us. When we get that, we can be quite irritating.

Speak truth. That's all. Then we should get out of the way.

What should I do now to put legs on what you've written, assuming that I agree with you?

Go out and offend someone so that uptight Christians and misinformed pagans will doubt your salvation.

Endnotes

Chapter 1: Halloween Horror

1. Link: http://home.ourladyoflourdesdaytona.com/all-are-welcome. Original credit: Rev. John Petty, All Saints Lutheran Church, Aurora, CO.

2. Dave Eggers, *The Circle* (Toronto: Alfred A. Knopf-Canada and San Francisco: McSweeney Books, 2013).

3. Mother Teresa, *A Simple Path* (New York: Random House, 1995), 79–80.

Chapter 2: Ugly in a Nudist Colony

1. Baltasar Gracian, *Gracian's Manual: A Truth-Telling Manual and the Art of Worldly Wisdom,* translated by Martin Fischer (Springfield, IL: Charles C. Thomas, 1945), 120.

Chapter 3: I've Gotta Be Me

1. Brennan Manning (with John Blasé), *All Is Grace* (Colorado Springs, CO: David C. Cook Publishers, 2011), 20–21.

2. Rick Warren, *The Purpose Driven Life* (Grand Rapids: Zondervan, 2002), 1.

3. Jared Wilson, *The Pastor's Justification* (Wheaton, IL: Crossway, 2013), 112–13.

Chapter 4: The Devil's Trinity

1. Alexander Solzhenitsyn, *The Gulag Archipelago 1918–56* (London: The Harvill Press, 2003).

2. Edward T. Welch, *Shame Interrupted: How God Lifts the Pain of Worthlessness and Rejection* (Greensboro, NC: New Growth Press, 2012), 11.

3. C. S. Lewis, *The Problem of Pain* (New York: MacMillan Publishing Company, 1962), 58–59.

4. Paul David Tripp, *A Quest for More: Living for Something Bigger Than You* (Greensboro, NC: New Growth Press, 2008), 70.

Chapter 5: Names for the Nameless

1. Sermon posted on www.keylife.org on March 12, 2015.

Chapter 6: Dead Men (and Women) Do Tell Tales

1. From a letter to Sir Joshua Reynolds in *The Life of Samuel Johnson, LL.D.*, 1824.

2. Paul Zahl, *PZ's Panopticon: An Off-the-Wall Guide to World Religion* (Charlottesville, VA: Mockingbird Ministries, 2013), 12.

Chapter 7: Gotcha!

1. Jennifer Knapp, *Facing the Music: My Story* (New York: Howard Books, 2014).

Endnotes

Chapter 8: When Doctrine Sings the "Hallelujah Chorus"

1. Chuck Colson and Timothy George, "Flaming Truth," *Christianity Today* (February 2012, Vol. 56, No. 2), 45.

Chapter 9: When Hitting a Wall Feels Good

1. I said a good deal more in my book *When Your Rope Breaks* . . . and I'm not above pushing my books.

2. Robert Beames, *Cornered by Grace: Right Where You Need to Be* (Oro Valley, AZ: Kolos Press, 2015), 1–2.

Chapter 10: Therefore

1. George Weigel, "Lessons in Statecraft: Exploration of the Distinctive—and Distinctively Effective—Diplomacy of St. John Paul," *First Things*, May 2015, 30.

2. Frederick Buechner, *Telling Secrets* (New York: Harper Collins, 1991), 2.

Chapter 11: Family Secrets

1. Brennan Manning, *All Is Grace* (Colorado Springs, CO: David C. Cook, 2011), 25.

2. Rachel Held Evans, *Searching for Sunday: Loving, Leaving, and Finding the Church* (Nashville: Nelson Books, 2015), 256.

3. Tom Saunders, *Go Ahead—Kill Yourself! Save Your Family the Trouble* (Plantation, FL: Distinctive Publishing Corporation, 1991).

4. Ronald Rolheiser, *The Holy Longing: The Search for a Christian Spirituality* (New York: Image, Random House Publishers, 2014), 128–29.

Chapter 12: A New Kind of Family

1. William D. Hendricks, *Exit Interviews: Revealing Stories of Why People Are Leaving the Church* (Chicago: Moody Press, 1993), 280.

2. Quoted on the C. S. Lewis Institute website in a piece by Art Lindsley entitled, "C. S. Lewis on Humility," 10/8/12.

Chapter 13: Masks and Mission

1. Scott Sauls, *Jesus Outside the Lines* (Carol Stream, IL: Tyndale House Publishers, 2015), xxvi–xxvii.

2. Ibid., 120–21.

Are you tired of
"do more, try harder" religion?

Key Life has only one message, to communicate the radical grace of God to sinners and sufferers. Because of what Jesus has done, God's not mad at you.

···

KEY LIFE
God's not mad at you

···

On radio, in print, on CDs and online, we're proclaiming the scandalous reality of Jesus' good news of radical grace...leading to radical freedom, infectious joy and surprising faithfulness to Christ.

For all things grace, visit us at **KeyLife.org**